PLAY-READINGS

PLAY-READINGS

For School, Radio and Screen Tests

SELECTED AND EDITED

BY

LOUISE M. FRANKENSTEIN

SAMUEL FRENCH

NEW YORK   LOS ANGELES

SAMUEL FRENCH (CANADA) Ltd.   TORONTO

SAMUEL FRENCH Ltd.   LONDON

MANUFACTURED IN THE UNITED STATES OF AMERICA
BY THE VAIL-BALLOU PRESS, INC., BINGHAMTON, N. Y.

PREFACE

This collection of scenes and speeches has been brought together to answer a very definite demand. In the last two or three years especially, I have found an increasing number of both students and tried actors asking for scenes for either practise or test use. My experience in reading hundreds of plays in the Drama Book Shop in New York has made it only a matter of a little research in order to pull these rabbits out of my memory hat to fill the requests for guidance. The excerpts in this book are from well-known and particularly from modern playwrights. They can be used not only for practise in dramatic classes, but also for radio auditions and screen tests. These selections were made after consultation with drama school directors, and officials of both radio broadcasting and moving picture companies.

Naturally, in a book necessarily limited in length, the scenes and speeches are condensed, and a series of dots indicate my somewhat heartless "cuts." In the name of the future actors and actresses who may use this volume, I crave indulgence of the very fine writers represented here, and I wish to thank both them and their publishers for their necessary and kind co-operation. I should like to refer readers of this book to the Book List at the end, where they will find noted the plays used and their prices. Undoubtedly the reading of the entire play studied will clarify those subtleties which cannot be indicated in the short scenes reprinted. Moreover, a play which contains one good characterization will contain others.

The table of contents is arranged by character to simplify the location of just the scene which fits the individual case. The variety of types of scenes is as great as space permitted.

33447

The editor of this book acknowledges with pleasure the assistance and advice of the American Academy of Dramatic Arts, New York, and is gratified to learn that the volume will be used in its work with the students of this institution.

It would be ungrateful of me to close without noting here my thanks to Miss Marjorie Seligman, my associate in the Drama Book Shop, for her continual friendly advice and helpful suggestions.

LOUISE M. FRANKENSTEIN

CONTENTS

The letters "m" and "w" are used to indicate the words "man" and "woman".

FOR ONE MAN

AMERICAN DREAM [1]

by

GEORGE O'NEIL

DANIEL PINGREE, *living in New England in 1650, is discontented with the narrow life his family leads. He explains in this speech to his mother his vision of a greater America that he shall help to found.*

DANIEL. Ah, Mother, how often have I said . . . [what I hope for?] . . . To live for something I have been born with. And to me this is no wilderness. It is the place of fulfillment—an Eden, if you will, waiting for the return of the redeemed exile—the wise Adam. And I feel unborn deeds marvelously suspended in the air here. In a way, it seems always morning to me here, even when the sun goes as it is going now. (*He smiles at her.*) Do you understand that, Mother? I wish you could. Then you could know a great tranquillity—for having come here and having borne your sons toward the free future. To have that feeling of morning in your mind! What great good fortune to be a man at this time, to stand here at the beginning of the world's best years. What a sense it gives a man to move out there on the fields in the dawn, ploughing the loam, looking back at the sea which lies between us and the old world, saying as the plough turns its fresh furrows: "All that is done here will be new! It will take your children a long time to outlive this morning." . . .

. . . Yes!—Here, here I tell you, the right shall be done at last. Millions of men will live together as friends, yes, as lovers. I tell you that will happen here. The inner sadnesses which eat the soul shall waste the world no more. Here let the faithful earth be answered worthily in this moving dream it carries. Here there will be a state such as the world has never seen. This is the land. . . . Here will the seasons move to feed the earth; long summers standing by to give us ease and heavy harvest. Now let men stand, each a pillar to the dream that feeds all space. Here—in this land, at last—men shall step into the sun. . . .

NO MORE FRONTIER [1]

by

TALBOT JENNINGS

FLINT BAILEY, *the speaker, is now an old man who has developed his ranch Hardtrigger (in Idaho) from its wilderness state. His son* GEORGE *has now seen fit to help in having the ranch condemned as a government dam site, but old* FLINT's *signature is necessary to consummate the deal. The old pioneer is not very proud of his son.*

FLINT. George, when Jim and I first came on this place, the Indians ran off our horses. Jim pulled down on 'em but his trigger stuck. That named our ranch [Hardtrigger], and it named our brand. A lot of things have happened here since '77, but one way or another every year the brand irons smoked on Hardtrigger. Now you want me to throw 'em in the lake. No more irons—Christ Almighty—no more irons. [And now] you['ve] sold [Hardtrigger]? You come to me and say, "Look here, Flint Bailey, we can use this land for a storage lake and we want to buy it." I say, "This

[1] Copyright, 1930, by Talbot Jennings.
Copyright, 1931, by Samuel French.

land's a cattle ranch and you can go to hell." You go to Congress and lobby around that Flint Bailey has a reservoir site but he won't sell. The Congressman says, "Re-elect me, and I'll buy Bailey's land." Then you hurry out here in a gas-wagon and tell me you've sold my land and I can get out or drown. If it's sold, that's the way you sold it.—(*In a moment he goes on.*) You tell me I've got to go. Where the hell can I go? I can't fly in the air; I can't live under the lake. Damn it, there *is* no place to go. [Go into town?] . . . Are you God Almighty? Did you make this country? You tell *me* to go to town! . . . You let [the engineers try to drive me out. I'm going to fight] . . . You're damn right I'm [going to fight]. (*A shaft of evening sunlight strikes his face. He turns abruptly and goes to the window. . . . FLINT walks to the fireplace and looks up at a pair of long-horns mounted on the chimney. Then he comes slowly back to the table.*) No, I won't fight. Thirty years ago I'd fight—five years ago. Not now—where's your papers? . . .

HOLIDAY [1]

by

PHILIP BARRY

NICK, *the speaker, is one of those happily gifted persons who, when at a cocktail party and surrounded by good friends, can be just as mad as the best man there. His speech is produced impromptu, like a rabbit out of a hat.*

NICK. You ask me for the story of my success?—Well, I'll tell you . . . Come—gather close, children. . . . I arrived in this country at the age of three months, with nothing in my pockets but five cents and an old hat-check. I

[1] Copyright, 1928 and 1929, by Philip Barry.

had no friends, little or no education, and sex to me was still the Great Mystery. But when I came down the gang-plank of that little sailing-vessel—steam was then unknown, except to the very rich— Friends, can you picture that manly little figure without a tug at your heart strings, and a faint wave of nausea? But I just pulled my belt a little tighter, and told myself "Don't forget you're a Potter, Nick"—I called myself "Nick"—and so I found myself at my first job, in the glass works. Glass was in its infancy then—we had barely scratched the surface—but I have never shirked work—and if there was an errand to be run, I ran five errands. If someone wanted to get off at the third floor, I took him to the tenth floor.—Then one day came my big chance. I was in the glass-blowing department then —now Miss Murphy's department—and a very capable little woman she is— . . . Oh, yes you are, Miss Murphy! Well, sir, I was blowing glass like a two-year-old, whistling as I blew. Suddenly I looked down and found in my hand—*a bottle*—or what we now know as a bottle. I rushed to my employer, a Mr. Grandgent, and said, "Look, Mr. Grand-gent—I think I've got something here." Mr. Grandgent looked—and laughed—*laughed,* do you understand?—I went from city to city like some hunted thing, that laugh still in my ears. But with me went my bottle. They called it Potters' Folly. They said it would never work. Well, time has shown how right they were. Now the bottle is in every home. I have made the bottle a National Institution!— And that, my dears, is how I met your grandmother. (*He bows.*) . . .

CYRANO DE BERGERAC [1]

by

EDMOND ROSTAND
Translated by Howard Thayer Kingsbury

CYRANO, *the adventurer, famed for his monstrous nose, has been twitted about that feature by a bored young noble looking for a bit of sport. When* CYRANO *replies, the dandy finds he has received more than he bargained for. The innocent remark which starts the tirade is* "You-your nose is-nose is-very large."

CYRANO.   No, young man.
That is somewhat too brief. You might say— Lord!—
Many and many a thing, changing your tone,
As for example these;—Aggressively:
"Sir, had I such a nose I'd cut it off!"
Friendly: "But it must dip into your cup.
You should have made a goblet tall to drink from."
Descriptive: " 'Tis a crag—a peak—a cape!
I said a cape?—'tis a peninsula."
Inquisitive: "To what use do you put
This oblong sheath; is it a writing-case
Or scissors-box?" Or, in a gracious tone:
"Are you so fond of birds, that like a father
You spend your time and thought to offer them
This roosting-place to rest their little feet?"
Quarrelsome: "Well, sir, when you smoke your pipe
Can the smoke issue from your nose, without
Some neighbor crying, 'the chimney is a-fire'?"

[1] From the original prompt book of Richard Mansfield through the courtesy of Mrs. Mansfield and the Smithsonian Institute.
Reprinted by permission of Howard Thayer Kingsbury, and by the courtesy of Mrs. Richard Mansfield.

Warning: "Be careful, lest this weight drag down
Your head, and stretch you prostrate on the ground."
Tenderly: "Have a small umbrella made,
For fear its color fade out in the sun."
Pedantic: "Sir, only the animal
Called by the poet Aristophanes
'Hippocampelephantocámelos'
Should carry so much flesh and bone upon him!"
Cavalier: "Friend, is this peg in the fashion?
To hang one's hat on, it must be convenient."
Emphatic: "Magisterial nose, no wind
Could give thee all a cold, except the mistral."
Dramatic: " 'Tis the Red Sea when it bleeds!"
Admiring: "What a sign for a perfumer!"
Poetic: "Is't a conch; are you a Triton?"
Naïve: "When does one visit this great sight?"
Respectful: "Let me, sir, pay my respects.
This might be called fronting upon the street."
Countrified: "That's a nose that is a nose!
A giant turnip or a baby melon!"
Or military: "Guard against cavalry!"
Practical: "Will you put it in a raffle?
It surely, sir, would be the winning number!"
Or parodying Pyramus, with a sob:
"There is the nose that ruins the symmetry
Of its master's features; the traitor blushes for it."
My friend, that is about what you'd have said
If you had had some learning or some wit;
But wit, oh! most forlorn of human creatures,
You never had a bit of; as for letters
You only have the four that spell out "Fool"!
Moreover, had you owned the imagination
Needed to give you power, before this hall,
To offer me these mad jests—all of them—
You would not even have pronounced the quarter
O' the half of one's beginning, for I myself

Offer them to myself with dash enough,
But suffer no one else to say them to me.

AS YOU LIKE IT

by

WILLIAM SHAKESPEARE

The hungry ORLANDO *wandering in the forest comes upon the* DUKE *and his court, chief member of which is the philosophical jester* JAQUES. *The* DUKE *comments that* "the universal theatre" *presents a more woeful spectacle than his own misfortune. To which* JAQUES *replies;*

JAQUES. All the world's a stage,
And all the men and women merely players:
They have their exits and their entrances;
And one man in his time plays many parts,
His acts being seven ages. At first, the infant,
Mewling and puking in the nurse's arms;
And then, the whining school-boy, with his satchel,
And shining morning face, creeping like snail
Unwillingly to school; And then, the lover;
Sighing like furnace, with woeful ballad
Made to his mistress' eye-brow: Then, a soldier;
Full of strange oaths, and bearded like the pard,
Jealous in honour, sudden and quick in quarrel,
Seeking the bubble reputation
Even in the cannon's mouth: And then, the justice;
In fair round belly, with good capon lined,
With eyes severe, and beard of formal cut,
Full of wise saws and modern instances,
And so he plays his part: The sixth age shifts
Into the lean and slippered pantaloon;
With spectacles on nose, and pouch on side;

His youthful hose, well saved, a world too wide
For his shrunk shank; and his big manly voice,
Turning again toward childish treble, pipes
And whistles in his sound: Last scene of all,
That ends this strange eventful history,
Is second childishness, and mere oblivion;
Sans teeth, sans eyes, sans taste, sans everything.

FOR ONE WOMAN

THE ROYAL FAMILY [1]

by

GEORGE S. KAUFMAN AND EDNA FERBER

JULIE, *star of stars is home from a* "dreadful matinee" (*and how she loves it!*). *This fact, plus the difficulty of getting her scapegrace brother,* TONY, *off to Europe quickly bring out her true form.* TONY *is a movie star who has punched his director's nose and fled Hollywood.*

(JULIE *enters. She is wearing smart winter street clothes— a luxurious fur coat and a costume to match. There is a bristling sort of vigor in the way she stations herself in the doorway. . . . Talks as she enters.*) . . .

JULIE. . . . What a dandy day this has been! . . . The entire population of New York is standing on the doorstep, howling for a glimpse of America's foremost screen lover. In the meantime they take what fortune sends, and it just so happened to be me. (*Sits on sofa. . . .*)—I had to get out at the corner—you don't dare drive up. And my dear Mrs. Cavendish, have you ever played to an audience made up entirely of sea lions! (*She is energetically tearing off hat, coat, kicks off her shoes.* DELLA, *meantime, comes down with mules. During* JULIE's *speech she kneels and assists her with slippers, etc.*) They came in wet to the knees and never did dry off. They spent the first act taking galoshes off and the last act putting them on. *You* know—— (*Stoops*

13

to pull imaginary zippers.)—I looked out once during the
last act and couldn't see a face. And cough! I think they
had a cheer leader. Lincoln couldn't have held them with
the Gettysburg address. . . . Tony, my love, Wolfe is
bringing [your passport].

. . . He's been pulling all sorts of wires. He's been in and
out of my dressing room all afternoon. *Everybody's* been in
and out of my dressing room all afternoon. Compared to
my dressing room, Grand Central Terminal was a rustic re-
treat. And all on account of you, my baby. Reporters, and
process servers, and sob sisters. . . . (*Lies on sofa.*). . . And
he's bringing the money for you, too. They kept your
reservation, and I've paid for it. You neglected to tell me
that you were roughing it across in the royal suite. . . .
Hire a battleship for all I care! But remember I'm a working girl. What do you do with all your money, anyway?
You go out to Hollywood with a billion dollar contract
and you buy a pink plaster palace for one hundred and fifty
thousand, an Isotta Fraschini for twenty thousand and an
Hispano Suiza for twenty-five, a camp in the Sierras for
another fifty—good God, you were sunk a quarter of a
million before they ever turned a crank on you! . . . And
as soon as they start to take a picture you knock out the
director and quit. . . .

THE NUT FARM [1]

by

John C. Brownell

The entire BENT *family transplants itself from Newark
into Hollywood, mostly because* HELEN *yearns to be a movie*

[1] Copyright, 1928, by John Charles Brownell (under the title of "It's the
Climate").
Copyright, 1930, by Samuel French.

star. After pushing herself as far as possible her chance comes, and she breaks the news to her husband.

HELEN. (*Goes to table; takes out photos from envelope; admires them as* BOB *watches her. She goes left to mirror.* BOB *comes down center. She sees him in mirror; turns, rushes to him, throws her arms about him and kisses him several times. Rapidly.*) Oh, Bob darling—I'm so glad you're home. I've missed you so, dear. I've so much to tell you. Oh, the most wonderful thing has happened, Bob. You never could guess it in a thousand years! I'm so happy I could cry! Oh, Bob—I'm going to make a lot of money for you, darling. I'm going to be of real value to you as a helpmate. We're going to be rich! *Rich,* sweetheart—and you're never going to have another worry in the world! Oh, I've met the most wonderful people since you've been away—influential people—and I've told them *all about you.* Sit down, dearest, and let little wifie pifie kneel beside you and tell you all about everything! (*She pushes the dazed* BOB *into chair right of table and kneels beside him.*) I've got talent, Bob—I have what they call at the studio—the *divine fire!* . . . I'm to be a star, Bob—think of it—a star! . . . With one picture we are going to triple our money, and then you can buy the kind of farm you want to buy. We needn't live on it right away, of course—for I'll have to make other pictures. The *public* will *demand them!* (. . . HELEN *rises suddenly and looks about.*) Wait till I show you those photographs. Oh, here they are. (*On floor up left center. Picks them up, opens the envelope and takes them out.*) Look at those, darling. Look at your little wifie pifie. Isn't she booful? The photographer said I look like Lillian Russell looked at eighteen. . . . And think of it—I might have never known I had real talent if I hadn't had the most *fortunate* meeting with one of the *great* impresarios of the film world, *Hamilton T. Holland!* All his associates at the Holland Studio think I'm lucky to have him take an interest in me. He *made* Mary

Pickford, they say—but he's real modest about it and won't claim *any* of the *credit*. Think of it! He says I am an emotional find, the Sarah Bernhardt of the screen! . . . Oh, I'm so happy, dear—aren't you?

DANGEROUS CORNER [1]

by

J. B. Priestley

MARTIN, *a supposed suicide, was beloved of a group of friends who mourn his loss. Gradually, intimate revelations show* MARTIN *to have been murdered by* OLWEN, *who in this speech, shares her knowledge.*

OLWEN. He took some [of this drug] while I was there and it had a terrible effect on him. It gave him a sort of devilish gaiety. I can see him now. His eyes were queer. Oh—he really wasn't sane. . . . I've tried not to think about it. He knew I disliked him, but he was so frightfully conceited that he couldn't believe it. He seemed to think that everybody young, male or female, ought to be falling in love with him. He saw himself as a sort of Pan. . . . He began taunting me. He thought of me or pretended to—as a priggish spinster, full of repressions, who's never really lived. All rubbish, because I'm really not that type at all. But he pretended to think I was and kept telling me that my dislike of him showed that I was trying to repress a great fascination he had for me. And of course that all these repressions were bad for me. I'd never lived, never would live, and all the rest of it. He talked a lot about that. I ought to have run out and left him, but I felt I couldn't

[1] Copyright, 1932, by J. B. Priestley.

while he was in that state. In a way I was sorry for him, because really he was ill, sick in mind and body, and I thought perhaps I could calm him down. I might dislike him, but after all he wasn't a stranger. He was one of our own set, mixed up with most of the people I liked best in the world. I tried to stop him. But everything I said seemed to make him worse. I suppose it would when he was in that excited abnormal state. Well, he talked about my repressions, and when I pretended to laugh at him, he got more and more excited. And then he tried to show me some beastly foul drawings he had—horrible obscene things by some mad Belgian artist— . . . He was different. He was ill. . . .

. . . There isn't a lot to tell you. When I pushed his beastly drawings away and was rather indignant about them, he got still more excited, completely unbalanced, and shouted out things about my repressions. And then I found he was telling me to take my clothes off. . . . I told him not to be a fool and that I was going. But then he stood between me and the door. And he had a revolver in his hand and was shouting, something about danger and terror and love. He wasn't threatening me with it or himself. He was just waving it about—being dramatic. I didn't even believe it was loaded. . . . But by this time I'd had more than enough of him—I couldn't be sorry for him any more —and I told him to get out of the way. When he wouldn't, I tried to push him out of the way. And then we had a struggle. He tried to tear my clothes. We really fought one another. It was horrible. He wasn't any stronger than I was. I'd grabbed the hand with the revolver in it. I'd turned the revolver towards him. His finger must have been on the trigger. I must have given it a jerk. The revolver went off. Oh— Horrible— . . . horrible. I've tried and tried to forget that. If he'd just been wounded, I wouldn't have left him alone. But he wasn't. He was dead. . . .

THE SILVER CORD [1]

by

SIDNEY HOWARD

DAVID *and* ROBERT *are two sons whose lives are dominated by a possessive mother.* CHRISTINA, *who speaks, truly loves her husband* DAVID, *but cannot bear her mother-in-law's overweening control of a grown man. The mother has just forced* ROBERT *to break his engagement.*

CHRISTINA. (*She turns from* [DAVID,] *but only for a moment: she quickly glances round and immediately returns to him, goes very close to him, to an intimate position, her hand resting on his arm. She speaks collectedly, gravely, but with steadily increasing fervour.*) Have you ever thought what it would be like to be trapped in a submarine in an accident? I've learned to-night what that kind of panic would be like. I'm in that kind of a panic now, this minute. I've been through the most awful experience of my life to-night, and I've been through it alone. (*She makes a little pause.*) I'm still going through it alone. (*She withdraws her hand from his arm.*) It's pretty awful to have to face such things alone. . . . No, don't interrupt me. I've got to get this off my chest. Ever since we've been married I've been coming across queer rifts in your feeling for me, like arid places in your heart. Such vast ones, too! I mean, you'll be my perfect lover one day, and the next I'll find myself floundering in sand and alone, and you nowhere to be seen. (*She makes a retiring step and a half-turn from him.*) We've never been really married, Dave. Only now and then, for a little while at a time, between your retirements into your arid places. —I used to wonder what you did there. At first, I thought you did your work there. But you don't. Your work's in my part of your heart, what there is of my part. Then I decided the other was just No-Man's Land. And I thought: little by little, I'll encroach upon it and pour my love upon it, like water on the western desert, and make it flower here and bear fruit there. I thought: then he'll be alive, all free and all himself; not partly dead and tied and blind; not partly someone else—or nothing. You see, our marriage and your architecture were suffering from the same thing. They only worked a little of the time. I meant them both to work all the time. I meant you to work all the time and to win your way, *all* your way, Dave, to complete man-hood. And that's a good deal farther than you've got so far.—Then we came here and this happened with Hes-ter and your brother, and you just stepped aside and did nothing about it! You went to bed. You did worse than that. You retired into your private wastes and sat tight.—(*She turns fully to him again.*) I've shown you what you should do and you won't see it. (*Standing close to him and slightly above him—she grips his arm convul-sively.*) I've called to you to come out to me, and you won't come. (*She draws back her hand.*) So now I've discovered what keeps you. Your mother keeps you. It isn't No-Man's Land at all. It's your mother's land. Arid, sterile, and your mother's! You won't let me get in there. Worse than that, you won't let life get in there! Or she won't!—That's what I'm afraid of, Dave: your mother's hold on you. I've seen what she can do with Robert. And what she's done to Hester. I can't help wondering what she may not do with you and to me and to the baby. (*Falls on her knees above* DAVID.) That's why I'm asking you to take a stand on this business of Hester's, Dave. You'll never find the right any clearer than it is here. It's a kind of test case for me. Don't you see? What you decide about this is what you may, eventually, be expected to decide about—about our mar-riage. . . .

ANNA CHRISTIE [1]

by

Eugene O'Neill

ANNA, *sent by her seafaring father to be sheltered with inland cousins, leaves them in disgust for her father's ship. There she falls in love with* MAT BURKE *and he with her, but he decides she should not marry him. When* MAT *and her father start to argue over her destiny, she can contain herself no longer.*

ANNA. (. . . *Blazing out at them.*) You can go to hell, both of you! (*There is something in her tone [which arrests their attention] . . .*)You're just like all the rest of them—you two! Gawd, you'd think I was a piece of furniture! I'll show you! Sit down now! (*As they hesitate—furiously.*) Sit down and let me talk for a minute. You're all wrong, see? Listen to me! I'm going to tell you something—and then I'm going to beat it. . . . I'm going to tell you a funny story, so pay attention. . . . I've been meaning to turn it loose on him [*her father*] every time he'd get my goat with his bull about keeping me safe inland. I wasn't going to tell you, but you've forced me into it. What's the dif? It's all wrong anyway, and you might as well get cured that way as any other. (*With hard mocking.*) Only don't forget what you said a minute ago about it not mattering to you what other reason I got so long as I wasn't married to no one else. . . .

. . . First thing is, I want to tell you two guys something. You was going on 's if one of you had got to own me. But nobody owns me, see?—'cepting myself. I'll do what I please and no man, I don't give a hoot who he is, can tell me what to do! I ain't asking either of you for a living.

I can make it myself—one way or other. I'm my own boss.
So put that in your pipe and smoke it! . . .

. . . Living with you is enough to drive anyone off their
nut. Your bunk about the farm being so fine! Didn't I
write you year after year how rotten it was and what a
dirty slave them cousins made of me? What'd you care?
Nothing! Not even enough to come out and see me! That
crazy bull about wanting to keep me away from the sea
don't go down with me! You're like all the rest of 'em! . . .

. . . But one thing I never wrote you. It was one of them
cousins that you think is such nice people—the youngest
son—Paul—that started me wrong. . . . It wasn't none of
my fault. I hated him worse'n hell and he knew it. But he
was big and strong— . . . like you! . . .

. . . That was why I run away from the farm. That was
what made me get a yob as nurse girl in St. Paul. (*With a
hard mocking laugh.*) And you think that was a nice yob for
a girl, too, don't you? (*Sarcastically.*) With all them nice inland fellers yust looking for a chance to marry me, I s'pose.
Marry me? What a chance! They wasn't looking for
marrying. . . .

. . . I'm owning up to everything fair and square. I was
caged in, I tell you—yust like in yail—taking care of other
people's kids—listening to 'em bawling and crying day and
night—when I wanted to be out—and I was lonesome—
lonesome as hell! (*With a sudden weariness in her voice.*)
So I give up finally. What was the use? (. . . [*The two
men*] *are motionless and silent* [*as she looks from one to the
other*] . . . *The condemnation* [ANNA] *feels in their silence
goads* [*her*] *into a harsh, strident defiance.*) You don't say
nothing—either of you—but I know what you're thinking.
You're like all the rest! . . . And who's to blame for it,
(*Turning to her father.*) me or you? If you'd even acted
like a man—if you'd even been a regular father and had
me with you—maybe things would be different! . . .

THE LATE CHRISTOPHER BEAN [1]

by

SIDNEY HOWARD

I-pause

ABBY *the maid of all work, who speaks, was the only member of* DR. HAGGETT's *household who was truly sympathetic to the late* CHRISTOPHER BEAN. *He was an impecunious young artist of no great repute (till after his death), but* ABBY *loved him and was good to him. She tells one of his friends what he did for her. (The man she speaks to is an impostor, but she does not know it at the time of this speech.)*

ABBY. He was the only man that ever took me serious and talked to me. He didn't talk so much. But what he said was awful pithy. And to think of you being Bert Davis! It certainly is a pleasure to make your acquaintance! I never expected to meet up with you. Don't you think we better shake hands on it? (*They do.*) Set down, Mr. Davis, and I'll set down with you. Mrs. Haggett don't favor the help setting in the setting room, but she's cityfied that way. And she ain't home anyhow and what she don't know won't hurt her. (*Her eyes shine as they take him in.*) Bert Davis! My, don't that name bring things back, though! . . . (*Nodding with [reminiscent] delight.*) Oh, yes, I liked [his painting]! Oh, I had to learn to like it. But he taught me. Oh, he taught me lots! And there wasn't nothing about him I didn't like! . . . Oh, [and] he taught me! Not that he set up to be a teacher. But you couldn't be with him and not pick up a mite here and a mite there. . . . Oh, I remember [so much]! It was mostly things to see, I guess.

[1] Founded upon "Prenez Garde a la Peinture" by Rene Fauchois.
Copyright, 1932, by Sidney Howard (under the title of "Muse of All Work").
Copyright, 1933, by Sidney Howard.

Like the rust color the marshes get this time of year when the sky gets the color of that old blue platter. (*She points to the platter on the cabinet shelf, adding proudly.*): That's cobalt blue! That's a painting term, cobalt blue! (*She continues.*) And he showed me the old red barn and the covered bridge that he was forever painting and I was used to all my life and never noticed. And he taught me that old chairs may be more than just old chairs to be thrown away. That some of 'em may be real beautiful. He used to say those very words about the old doors in the brick houses up along the common! That was when they begun taking the old doors out and putting in new ones ordered from Sears Roebuck. And did you know that old brick houses ain't red but mostly green and brown and that moonlight and snow ain't white at all but all kinds of colors and that elm trees is most decorative when their leaves comes off? That's another painting term, decorative. He taught me! (*Her reminiscence becomes more personal.*) He taught me that a man can get drunk and not be no different only just more so and that everybody's got more good qualities than bad. Oh, he taught me lots! And I ain't never forgot none of it. I lived over and over that time he spent here. Over and over it ever since he died. . . .

TORCH SONG [1]

by

KENYON NICHOLSON

IVY, *now a Salvation Army lassie, was once a torch singer in a night club.* HOWARD, *a traveling salesman, to whom she speaks had asked her to marry him, although he was engaged to his boss's daughter. One night, while* IVY *is singing,* HOWARD *is persuaded to leave her. He goes, and when*

[1] Copyright, 1930, by Kenyon Nicholson.

IVY *meets him several years later, she describes her emotions of that night.*

IVY. (*Clutching Bible to her.*) . . . After I got your note that night, it was like the bottom fell out of everything. I couldn't seem to get ahold of myself. (*Noticing his expression.*) Oh, don't feel bad—it's all over now; but at the time it left my life so empty—and nothing seemed to fill it. I moped around in that dingy rooming house for days, and one night when I was sitting in my room there was a knock on the door. It was Carl—standing there in his uniform. I'd seen him before—passed him in the hall. He asked if he could come in and talk to me. He'd heard me crying, I guess. Well, I let him talk, for I was pretty blue. From then on he got the habit of dropping in whenever he could—to cheer me up—I liked him from the first. —Well, it wasn't long till one evening he took me with him to their regular Wednesday services, in a hall down on Seventh Street. I sang hymns and listened to people testifying—and it did me a lot of good— Well, quite late that night Carl came in my room again. He sat there on my bed, telling me the wonderful things Salvation could do for me. I didn't take much stock in it at first, but then I figured if God could stop my pain, I would give myself to Him—work for Him all my life— I don't know to this day what happened exactly—but all of a sudden I felt weak and faint—like I was walking on air. I felt Jesus right in the room! "Jesus," I said, "I'm a sinner. Thou art the Saviour, I take Thee now to be my Saviour. I put my soul in Thy hands!"—That was all— And I knew that Christ with all his brightness and power had come into my heart—that the sorrows and temptations had passed away—I was different —new—clean! I was free! Oh, the feeling of safety and peace you get resting on Jesus! Oh, it was glorious, Howard! It's wonderful to have a birthday, but as Carl says, it's more wonderful to have *two* birthdays. And that's what happened to me, Howard. *I was born again!* . . .

TOMORROW AND TOMORROW [1]

by

PHILIP BARRY

GAIL *and his wife,* EVE, *have been discussing what their children will be like, although they have none as yet. During* EVE'S *speech* GAIL *slowly drops off to sleep.*

EVE. But I'm—I was an only child, you know. So was my mother. Maybe there's something wrong with me. . . . —Maybe I ought to find out if there is—but I dread to know it. (*Another silence.*)—I can't sleep for thinking of it. I don't know why I shouldn't have one. I'm quite strong. I've never had anything really the matter with me.—And I love children, I do love them. If loving children made you have them, I'd have a houseful.—And besides, I would so love the actual having of one. I shouldn't mind any kind of pain at all. I'd welcome it. I'd know then that I was living—making—and not slowly dying, a little more each day like this. (*Again* GAIL'S *chin has sunk upon his breast.* EVE'S *eyes are straight ahead, her voice low. A silence.*)—They must be even sweeter when they're all your own. There's nothing about them I don't like.—Even if it should be a girl—but of course it wouldn't be, not the first one. (*Another silence. Her voice becomes lower still.*)—Heaven shine on me, rain on me. Bring something out of me to hold in my arms, send me some small thing to care for. I'll love it tenderly. Only I shall look after it, ever. I shall become wise. I shall know what is good for him. I shall find out everything there is to know. Don't keep me empty this way any longer. I have room. I'm strong. I'm well. (*A longer silence. Then.*)—Listen to me, Gail: I'm speaking honestly: I must have a child, or in a while I shan't be good for anything at all. Help me to life, Gail. Hold fast to it with your strong hands and bring me to it—(*Blindly, she reaches her hand out to him. He does not take it. Slowly, she turns and looks at him. He is asleep. A silence. She drops her hand lifelessly into her lap. Then she speaks in another voice.*) Gail—(*And again.*)—Gail. . . .

MERCHANT OF VENICE

by

WILLIAM SHAKESPEARE

PORTIA, *the eloquent young woman lawyer, appeals to the jury.*

PORTIA. The quality of mercy is not strained;
It droppeth as the gentle rain from heaven,
Upon the place beneath: it is twice blessed:
It blesseth him that gives, and him that takes:
'Tis mightiest in the mightiest; it becomes
The thronèd monarch better than his crown:
His sceptre shows the force of temporal power,
The attribute to awe and majesty,
Wherein doth sit the fear and dread of kings;
But mercy is above the sceptered sway,
It is enthronèd in the hearts of kings,
It is an attribute to God himself;
And earthly power doth then show likest God's
When mercy seasons justice: therefore, Jew,
Though justice be thy plea, consider this,—
That, in the course of justice, none of us

Should see salvation. We do pray for mercy;
And that same prayer doth teach us all to render
The deeds of mercy; I have spoke thus much,
To mitigate the justice of thy plea;
Which, if thou follow, this strict court of Venice
Must needs give sentence 'gainst the merchant there.

FOR ONE MAN AND ONE WOMAN

ANOTHER LANGUAGE [1]

by

ROSE FRANKEN

STELLA *is a very charming young woman, who has married the most middle-class son of the middle-class Hallam family. When we find her she is hostess to* JERRY. *He is actually her nephew, but relationships do not count. These two speak another language, one which finds* JERRY'S *ambition to be an architect more stimulating than Hallam small chat.*

STELLA. Hello, Jerry—

(JERRY *pauses on the threshold. He seems strained and inwardly excited.*)

JERRY. Shall I put my things in the closet?

STELLA. You can just leave them—

(JERRY *throws his coat and hat over hall chair and enters room carrying a crisply wrapped package, which he keeps behind his back.*)

JERRY. (*Looking around.*) Gosh. The room's beautiful at night. This is the first time I've ever seen it at night, you know. With the candles and everything lit—

STELLA. Well, you sit here and enjoy it. I'm going to change my dress—

JERRY. (*Quickly.*) No don't—I like it, what you've got on— it makes you look so much taller than you really are—

STELLA. (*Matter-of-factly.*) Oh I'm pretty husky—

JERRY. (*With a small break.*) You're tiny. I could lift you up in one hand—

STELLA. Don't you believe it.

(*Puts her hand on bedroom door, meaning to go in.*)

JERRY. Stella,—please—I want to show you something—

STELLA. Show me later—

JERRY. I—don't want to show you later. When everyone's around. I kept imagining on the way down, me walking in, and you here by yourself—I didn't think it would happen —but it has—so you can't just go in and change your dress—

(*His voice falters; he looks at her beseechingly.*)

STELLA. (*After an instant's hesitation.*) Well—what is it, Jerry?

JERRY. (*Fumbling awkwardly with the package in his hand.*) I feel like a fool now. You didn't act this way on Saturday.

STELLA. Saturday?

JERRY. Gosh—don't you even remember?

STELLA. (*Aware of his overwrought condition, and careful to keep the scene casual.*) I remember that we went to the exhibition—

JERRY. Is that all?

STELLA. Why yes—

JERRY. I remember more than that. I remember every word you said—and how you looked when you said it—

STELLA. Jerry this is dreadful, you sound like a detective!

JERRY. No, I'm not fooling. Being with you that day made everything different and wonderful—but all it meant to you was—going to an exhibition I guess.

STELLA. Oh no, it didn't, it meant more than that, Jerry. Because I enjoyed seeing the pictures with you—it was nice being with someone for a change.—It was awfully nice.

(*There is a wistful, unguarded note in her voice as she adds the last sentence.* JERRY *is arrested by it, he searches her eyes eagerly. But* STELLA's *face has suddenly become a mask. She turns a friendly impersonal smile upon him. It quenches* JERRY's *fire. When he speaks again, the timbre has gone from his voice.*)

JERRY. Oh. Well. I see, sure. (*Turns away in disappointment.*) I'm just crazy, I guess. Forget it, will you, Stella? I came in here, just sort of crazy, that's all—

STELLA. (*Not disputing it.*) What was it you wanted to show me, Jerry?

JERRY. (*Very young, with his back to her.*) Nothing. It wouldn't mean anything to you. Never mind.

(*Turns half toward her, twanging the string of his package, as if he wishes she'd take it from him.*)

STELLA. (*Smiling.*) Is this it? (*Takes the package.*)

JERRY. (*In his throat.*) Umm.

STELLA. (*Uncertain.*) Shall I open it?

JERRY. (*Inarticulate.*) Sure. If—if you want.

STELLA. It's—soft!

(*A beautiful little grin comes over* JERRY's *tense young features.*)

JERRY. Go ahead. See what it is.

(STELLA *unwraps it, and brings to light an enchanting English puppy made of plush. It is at once nonsensical and appealing.*)

STELLA. (*Taken unawares.*) Oh! [That plush puppy!]

JERRY. (*His face transfigured.*) Do you remember it?

STELLA. Of course I remember it— (*She has forgotten* JERRY, *forgotten the dog; her mind is in some hinterland of space.*) We were walking over Fifty-seventh Street—after the exhibition—it was in a shop window—

JERRY. (*Taking it swiftly, and with laughter.*) And you were like a little kid, the way you stopped and laughed at it—

STELLA. I've always had a weakness for toy-stores—

JERRY. (*His voice trembling with happiness.*) And you said —"Oh, Jerry, Look! Isn't it adorable!"—and I knew right away that I'd have to surprise you with it!

STELLA. (*Turning her eyes upon him as if she has come back from a long distance; speaking slowly.*) But you shouldn't have done it, Jerry—

JERRY. D-don't you like it?

STELLA. I love it. It's one of the sweetest things that ever happened to me, your surprising me this way. But it won't do, you see. (*She tries to smile.*) It just won't do.

JERRY. Why you're crying!

STELLA. Nonsense! Why should I cry—over a funny little dog?

JERRY. (*At a loss; his eyes wide.*) I don't *know!*

STELLA. . . . [*Smiling.*] Neither do I. . . .

ONE SUNDAY AFTERNOON [1]

by

JAMES HAGAN

BIFF, *the husband, has just been released from two years in prison. It is a spring night, and his wife* AMY, *having failed to meet him at the station has come hopefully to the spot in the park where they used to meet as sweethearts.*

BIFF. (*Quietly.*) Hello, Amy.

AMY. (*Rising from bench.*) Biff.

BIFF. Yep—it's me. (*Pause. She rocks a little.*) What are you doing— (*Pause.* AMY *sits.*) Just goin' over to the house. Dropped off at the junction. Could have made the five-forty-five but I didn't want anybody at the station to see me.

AMY. (*Quietly.*) I know—

BIFF. (*Sheepishly.*) Something told me you would be here —don't know, just something. (*Pause.*) Nice over here to-night—spring.

AMY. Yes—spring.

BIFF. Smells good—the earth—the trees. Everything seems to be waking up. New life coming in. (*There is an awkward pause.* BIFF *whistles softly and walks a little.*) Got out at twelve o'clock. The Warden was a prince of a chap. Shook hands and—and—(*Pause. He is near her.*) Glad to see me, Amy?

AMY. You know I am, Biff.

BIFF. (*Sits—not too near her.*) Feels good to see you—feels good to be back. Two years—(*Looking round.*) Seems more like ten.

AMY. Biff—I'm so glad to see you.

BIFF. Same here— Guess I would have been all shot to pieces if I hadn't gotten your letters. The thought of you waiting —I just somehow—somehow—(*There is a break in his voice—he catches himself.*)

AMY. It's all right, Biff.

BIFF. (*Laughs.*) I knew you would be waiting over here— s' funny—(*He takes her hand and holds it.*) Thank you, Amy, for all your kindness,—all your goodness.

AMY. That's all right, Biff.

BIFF. You all right, Amy? (*Laughs.*)

AMY. Yes—I'm all right, Biff—it was just seeing you—

BIFF. Sure, I understand— . . . Learned a lot since I've been away—

AMY. Yes—

BIFF. S' funny—the same moon; the same stars, the same rain comes down on us all. It doesn't know whether you're a crook or an angel—a cock-eyed Chinaman— It doesn't give a damn. It just says "Here I am—I'm yours, what the hell are you going to do about it?"—it's good too. It never gives any pain or heartaches—there isn't any worry in it. Never takes anything from you but gives everything. (*Pause.*) You know, Amy—there's a lot of good in people if we look for it. The trouble is—we don't look for it. We just go through life saying "I'm O.K. and the other guy is all wrong."—When you lie in a bunk at night with nothing but men around—it is different—you can feel it. There seems to be an understanding.

AMY. I know, Biff.

BIFF. Sure you do—you always know. (*He pats her hand.*) Quiet—isn't it?

AMY. Yes—(*The gramophone is heard playing "Let the rest of the world go by."*)

BIFF. Wonder who's got that music box going?

AMY. It's coming from that house over yonder. (*Both listen.*)

BIFF. What's it playing—something new, isn't it?

AMY. Yes—"Let the rest of the world go by"—

BIFF. (*Dreamily.*) "Let the rest of the world go by"— (*Rises. . . .*) Guess we'll have to let this town go by, Amy.

AMY. All right, Biff—

BIFF. O.K. with you?

AMY. Wherever you go, Biff—I'll go.

BIFF. Ought to take us a day to pack—I'll go over to Hillsdale and make arrangements.

AMY. All right.

BIFF. (*Laughs.*) There's something big coming up for Biff Grimes and his wife. I can feel it in my bones—Biff Grimes is going to be Biff Grimes—Yessir—there ain't going to be nothing too good for Biff Grimes and his family—God, it feels good! (*Pause. He holds out his arms.*) Want to go home, honey?

AMY. Yes—

BIFF. All right. (AMY *rises*—BIFF *turns to her—then takes her in his arms.*) I love you, Amy—I think you are the loveliest lady in the world. I love your hair—your eyes—your mouth—

AMY. (*Looking up at him.*) I love you too, Biff— (*They kiss.*)

BIFF. (*Looking up.*) Look at that old sky—must be a million stars out—Moon is full up—

AMY. Yes—

BIFF. Spring—let's walk home. . . .

SECRETS [1]

by

RUDOLF BESIER AND MAY EDGINTON

JOHN CARLTON, *in love with* MARY, *against the wishes of her stern father, comes by ladder to her room one night and tells her they must break from her home and elope to America.* MARY *has a deep courage, and although her respect for her father is great, her love and trust in* JOHN *is greater. The year is 1867.*

JOHN. . . . Now, darling, my plan. . . . Mary, a ship sails for America in three days' time. I found out this afternoon that I can get passages for both of us. . . .

MARY. . . . America?

JOHN. Yes. . . .We can't get married before we land on the other side. Till then you *know*—you will be sacred—I wouldn't so much as touch your little finger if it offended you— You know that?

MARY. Yes, John.

JOHN. . . . By running away with me your family will consider that you have disgraced them and utterly disown you. You will have nobody in the world to depend upon but me. And I'm only—

MARY. . . . Nobody but you! You're all I want— Now, and to the end of my life.

JOHN. . . . Mary!

MARY. . . . And I'll follow you to the end of the world.

JOHN. No—no! . . . You don't realize—you can't. . . . You'll have to cook—you'll have to sew.—You'll— You'll— . . .

MARY. . . . Yes, John.

JOHN. Darling, listen. For years and years I shall be a poor man—a—a working man—and you'll be a poor woman—a working woman. . . . All you'll have is my love and my *love* and my *love*—but you'll suffer—you'll— Are you listening, dear?—Do you understand?

MARY. . . . Yes, John. . . . It sounds all—so beautiful!

JOHN. Beautiful, you angel? But think of all it means— Mary, do you realize that for years and years I shall never be able to give you a dress like this?

MARY. What do dresses matter?

JOHN. They don't matter. They shan't matter till I can give them to you myself. . . . Mary, Mary—say you believe in me and love me, say you believe in me.—

MARY. . . . I love you, John—I love you and I believe in you. . . . John, when did you say the ship sails?

JOHN. On Thursday.

MARY. But papa's taking me to visit Uncle and Aunt for a week tomorrow. . . .

JOHN. . . . Then you must come away with me tonight . . . Now.

MARY. . . . Now? But, John, . . . the door's locked.

JOHN. You'll have to leave by the window. . . . I'll help you down.

MARY. (*In a small voice, but with no hesitation in it.*) Very well, John.

JOHN. . . . And you can't possibly go in that dress. You must change it.

MARY. . . . Change it? Now?

JOHN. Quick, dear, quick. . . .

MARY. Very well, John. . . .

JOHN. . . . Here, let me . . . It's all right, dear. Look on me as your lady's-maid. I'm the only one you're likely to have for the Lord knows how long. . . . As for me—when your father finds you've vanished—confound these hooks and things!—he'll make a bee-line for my lodgings. I must clear out of them tonight. . . . [I'll give my landlady to understand that I'm going to Scotland.] . . . There, that's done. . . . Is that the dress, dear?

MARY. Yes, John.

JOHN. . . . How does it go on?

MARY. It—it has to go over my head.

JOHN. I understand. Of course. . . . You see, darling, this is the first time I've ever dressed a girl.

MARY. . . . Is it, John? . . .

JOHN. . . . Yes, . . . and now you'll leave a note for your father. . . .

MARY. But—John—

JOHN. Pen and ink and paper. Quick!

MARY. But, John—

JOHN. Sit down and write. . . . "Dear Papa—I've gone to Scotland to marry John . . ." (*She writes.*)

MARY. . . . But that's not true, John.

JOHN. . . . Of course it isn't or I wouldn't ask you to write it.

MARY. Oh, John, I told him I would never deceive him again.

JOHN. . . . You've got to.

MARY. . . . Got to? You—command me to do it, John?

JOHN. Yes, Mary.

MARY. (*A frightened, happy gasp.*) Oh! (*She goes on writing. He dictates.*)

JOHN. "I hope you will try to forgive—your loving daughter, Mary." . . . Just leave it there. . . . Come, darling. . . . It's not too late to draw back.

MARY. John dear—

JOHN. No, listen to me. I've told you a little of what's in store for you. But of myself I've said nothing. I'm not the man you think me. I'm hard and callous and brutal. What I want I take, whether it's right or wrong. I want you, so I'm taking you. But it's not too late. You can still—

MARY. . . . No, John. . . . You see, I love you; and even if you are all you say you are—I'd love you still. You want me—and that's all I ask.

JOHN. (*In a whisper.*) Mary. . . . Quick, darling, put out the candles. . . . You must go first. You'll be quite safe.

MARY. (*Tremulously.*) Y-yes, John. . . .

JOHN. I'll hold you firmly, darling, you needn't be afraid.

MARY. . . . I-I-I'm n-not in the l-least afraid, John. . . .

THE YOUNG IDEA [1]

by

NOEL COWARD

JENNIFER *and* GEORGE, *after a divorce and separation of fif-teen years, are brought together by their conspiring chil-dren. In the period of their separation,* GEORGE *has remar-ried and been deserted by his wife, and* JENNIFER *has become affianced to an American.* GEORGE'S *second wife is the* CICELY *in question.*

JENNIFER. (*On settee; almost in tears.*) I shall never forgive . . . you for this——

GEORGE. Jennifer! . . .

JENNIFER. How dare you spring on me without any warn-ing—like—like a rattlesnake!!!

GEORGE. They made me come.

JENNIFER. (*Quickly.*) Then you didn't want to?

GEORGE. . . . You *know* I did.

JENNIFER. (*Crossly.*) Well, all I can say is, it's very incon-siderate.

GEORGE. (*Irately.*) It's nothing of the sort. It's a pleasant sur-prise.

JENNIFER. (*Rises.*) Pleasant! Huh! You ought to be ashamed of yourself! . . .

GEORGE. (*Quite cross.*) Why should I be ashamed just be-cause I love you still?

JENNIFER. Where's Cicely? . . .

GEORGE. Damn Cicely!

JENNIFER. I consider that remark in very bad taste. I suppose, when you first married Cicely, you used to damn Jennifer all day long!

GEORGE. . . . Cicely's left me for good and all. I shall never see her again.

JENNIFER. . . . Have you any aspirin on you?

GEORGE. No; I'm so sorry.

JENNIFER. I'm sure I shall have a headache in a minute. To have you suddenly reappearing like this is enough to unman any woman.

GEORGE. Don't trifle with me—don't be flippant. This is our first meeting after fifteen years. Let's treat it in the proper spirit.

JENNIFER. If only you'd given me a little warning, I could have worked myself up into the right atmosphere without the least trouble. I should have put a lamp in the window.

GEORGE. (*Appealingly.*) Jennifer!

JENNIFER. As it is, I'm taken utterly by surprise.

GEORGE. Let's wait to discuss it until later, when the shock has worn off a bit.

JENNIFER. Are you really so eager, then?

GEORGE. (*Crosses to* JENNIFER.) I want to come back here to you and the children more than anything in the world, Jennifer. (*He catches her hand.*) Don't be tiresome.

JENNIFER. Really, you are *amazing*! After living fourteen years with another woman, you drop out of a cloudless sky and call me tiresome.

GEORGE. Well, you are—thoroughly!

JENNIFER. Perhaps I am—rather. (*Sits on settee.*)

GEORGE. Jennifer—in a few months all the divorce business

will be settled,—and we're both getting on, you know,—we shan't be as Temperamental as we used to be.

JENNIFER. Nonsense! I shall always be Temperamental—that's just it. You jump at conclusions so. As a matter of fact, I'm ever so much worse than I was, having been left alone to do as I like.

GEORGE. (*Sits.*) I'm not afraid.

JENNIFER. If I agree to marry you again, I want you to understand that it will be solely on account of [the children].

GEORGE. Very well.

JENNIFER. And I should like to arrange things on a more or less business basis. We must make a list of the subjects that we cannot discuss calmly. (*Counting on her fingers.*) Religion, George Moore, Democracy, my novels——

GEORGE. (*Amiably.*) I won't criticize a word of your novels, if you don't want me to.

JENNIFER. I don't mind your criticisms, George, as long as they're sensible and enthusiastic.

GEORGE. Anything more?

JENNIFER. Certainly. You mustn't dominate me—I hate being dominated.

GEORGE. I never did.

JENNIFER. And you must never try to make me eat things I don't like—you always used to.

GEORGE. I didn't.

JENNIFER. Yes, you did. One of our fiercest quarrels started with Apple Pudding.

GEORGE. You were so faddy.

JENNIFER. Never mind; I like being faddy. (*Rises, crosses to center.*)

GEORGE. (*Meekly.*) All right.

JENNIFER. Promise me that you won't persuade me to live in England for good.

GEORGE. I promise. (*Rises, to center.*)

JENNIFER. And, above all things, you must never become reminiscent about Cicely.

GEORGE. You will want to talk about Cicely more than I shall.

JENNIFER. Oh no, I shan't!

GEORGE. Won't you say "Yes" or "No" now?

JENNIFER. There you go, dominating me! (*Sits.*)

GEORGE. Will you answer one question?

JENNIFER. That depends. What is it?

GEORGE. Do you care for me at all—any more?

JENNIFER. I suppose I do, really, but still, that doesn't settle things by any means. I had to crush down so much unhappiness fifteen years ago that—do you know, I believe I crushed all my capacity for happiness with it also. The fact of our caring for one another didn't prevent our quarrelling before.

GEORGE. We're older now.

JENNIFER. I know. There's no need to keep harping on it.

GEORGE. You're much too sensible to mind growing old.

JENNIFER. Am I? I wonder!

GEORGE. I know. Once we're together again, it won't matter a bit. There's such a lot of happiness waiting for us just round the corner—if only we're careful.

JENNIFER. Perhaps!

GEORGE. (*Going towards her.*) Jennifer—you are a darling.

JENNIFER. (*Rises, warding him off.*) George, it's too late. That poor American—I've given my word.

GEORGE. He released you from it. (*To center.*)

JENNIFER. Only because he was cross. I can't let him go all the way back to Chicago by himself.

GEORGE. He'll have to. He doesn't love you as much as I do.

JENNIFER. More, I'm afraid. You see, not having been married to me before, he doesn't know of my disadvantages.

GEORGE. (*Firmly.*) I'm sorry, but he'll have to do without you.

JENNIFER. (*Horrified.*) George, how can you be so selfish?

GEORGE. I love you.

JENNIFER. So does he, and you're calmly suggesting that I should break his heart!

GEORGE. (*Unmoved.*) Yes.

JENNIFER. No, George,—on second thoughts, I'm afraid. (*Sits at desk.*)

GEORGE. Stop, stop! Don't go any longer—I won't have it. I know you, and I can see through you. You determined in your own mind to have me back the very first moment you saw me, and you're prevaricating and arguing just to keep me on the rack. This is one of the most delightful moments in your life, and you're revelling in it at the cost of my peace of mind. You love me—it's no use pretending you don't, because every nerve and instinct I possess is screaming that you do—you do! You only tolerated the thought of that wretched American at all on account of the children. You love me! You love me! You've wanted me all these years, as much as I have wanted you. The sight of you has completely annihilated the time we've been parted. The only thing in the world that matters is Youth. And I've got it back again. I'm twenty-one, and I want to laugh and shout and tear the house down! Come and kiss me!

JENNIFER. (*Going to him.*) George! You haven't altered a bit!

LET US BE GAY [1]

by

RACHEL CROTHERS

BOB *and* KITTY *have been divorced at her firm demand when she learns he has been philandering. Both wander over the world for years,* KITTY *outwardly much changed from the mousy housewife she once was. They meet again at a houseparty where each tries to arouse the other's jealousy. Finally they are alone for an intimate talk.*

KITTY. (*Letting her feeling carry her away at last.*) Heaven and earth and *God* were all mixed up in *you*. When that was gone *nothing* was left. Can't you understand that? I suppose you think I ought to have stayed at home with a broken heart, for the rest of my life—hugging my ideals. But I didn't seem to be able to do that. I had to get out and find out what it was all about—to see why *you* did it.

BOB. Well, then if you've found out so much—if you've got so wise and experienced—you know now how little that affair meant to me.

KITTY. Yes, I know now. I know both sides. I wanted to find out whether I'd been a fool or not—whether I had exaggerated what you did. Well, I hadn't. It was just as horrible as I thought it was. Bob, marriage means just one thing—complete and absolute fidelity or it's the biggest farce on *earth*.

[1] Copyright, 1929, by Rachel Crothers.

BOB. I could make our marriage now what you thought it ought to be then.

KITTY. (*Sitting on the sofa at left.*) That I should live to hear you say that, Mr. Brown!

BOB. (*Standing in front of her.*) How can you be so hard?

KITTY. Because I refuse to be made unhappy again.

BOB. (*Sitting above her on the sofa.*) Kitty, darling—if you'd let me begin again! God—what we've lost! Two people who loved each other as we did! . . .
. . . Give me a chance to make you love me again. That's fair, isn't it?

KITTY. Love isn't enough, Bob.

BOB. The children.

KITTY. We *had* the children. We had love—but that didn't keep us together. No, Bob, I'm not going to give you a chance to hurt me again. *It's the awfullest hurt in the world* and it would still be there, if I'd let it. (*She rises and moves away from him.*)

BOB. (*Following her a little.*) But I *wouldn't* hurt you again.

KITTY. No, Bob—I'm not going back. I'm going *on*. I don't know to just *what*—but *on*. For heaven's sake let's be gay about it.

BOB. To see you like this is a worse tragedy than losing you. Aren't you sick of this damned batting around—trying to fool yourself into thinking you're having a good time?

KITTY. Maybe you've had enough—you've been at it longer than I have—maybe you're ready for your slippers at the fire—I'm not. (*Putting on her coat.*)

BOB. Oh, Kitty, marry me again.

KITTY. You're out of your senses.

BOB. It's what I want. It's the only thing I do want—you and the children. Can't we make a fresh start?

KITTY. It's too late.

BOB. Do you hate me?

KITTY. (*Putting on her gloves.*) No.

BOB. Then why—

KITTY. Oh, it isn't you.

BOB. What is it then?

KITTY. It's myself. I couldn't. Neither could you, Bob. You're just making a gallant gesture.

BOB. No. From the minute I saw you, something pounded in me so hard—an idiotic hope—a something bigger than I ever had—or ever knew there could be. . . .
     . . . Do you think I could make you love me again? That's the point.

KITTY. That's what I'm afraid of. That's why I'm running now.

BOB. (*Going to her.*) Kitty—

KITTY. If I let myself go, I could be fascinated by you again in no time at all.

BOB. You're adorable!

KITTY. (*Holding him off.*) No, Bob, let's not make fools of ourselves. It would be no joke for either one of us to try to settle down again.

BOB. But we—

KITTY. No, I'm afraid, Bob. I'm honestly *afraid*. . . .

BOB. Why? Why, dearest?

KITTY. I don't know. I've been so gay—so—so full of—so *empty*.

BOB. . . . Kitty!

KITTY. So lonely—

BOB. Darling!

KITTY. Oh, Bob, I love you so. . . . Take me back.

THERE'S ALWAYS JULIET [1]

by

JOHN VAN DRUTEN

DWIGHT, *an American man visiting in London on business, meets and instantly falls in love with* LEONORA. *He is unexpectedly called back to the United States, and the two part somewhat unpleasantly,* LEONORA *refusing to marry* DWIGHT *because she is not sure she honestly loves him after knowing him only three days. Just before the scene opens he has phoned he is coming to see her, since he has not sailed.* (LEONORA'S *nickname is* STEVE.)

DWIGHT. Hello. (*He comes in.*)

LEONORA. (*As lightly as possible.*) What you come back for?

DWIGHT. (*Equally so.*) Business.

LEONORA. Business?

DWIGHT. Yes. When I got on board I found a cable . . . telling me to stay over and see a man who's just arrived in England.

LEONORA. Oh! I see!

DWIGHT. I got back around seven. . . . [*Pause.*] . . .

LEONORA. . . . How long are you staying this time?

[1] Copyright, 1931, by John van Druten.

DWIGHT. Till Saturday. The *Aquitania*. (*She laughs.*) What is it?

LEONORA. Another three days. It's—teasing.

DWIGHT. Yes.

LEONORA. (*Suddenly serious—almost hostile.*) What did you have to come back for?

DWIGHT. Do you mind?

LEONORA. I think I mind.

DWIGHT. Why?

LEONORA. Why? Because I hate anti-climax!

DWIGHT. (*Gently, after a pause, away from her.*) Steve, do you remember something you said to me the very first time I came here. . . .

LEONORA. What?

DWIGHT. You were explaining your friendship with Tom and Catherine. You said you played with them in the hope of finding some excitement that you knew you'd be too scared to take hold of if it offered.

LEONORA. Well?

DWIGHT. I gathered you didn't altogether like that side of yourself.

LEONORA. Well?

DWIGHT. Well—

LEONORA. You mean—you're the excitement?

DWIGHT. Yes.

LEONORA. I see.

DWIGHT. It doesn't do to be too sensible. It's a reaction against Victorianism. Reaction in the English sense, not the American. If you'd been a Victorian we'd have been off to—what's the name of the place—Gretna Green—the minute you let me kiss you. Victorian girls were always marrying men they didn't know a thing about. They called it romance. I'm all for romance myself.

LEONORA. (*Reflectively.*) Yes. Yes. Only I know a lot more about you than I did.

DWIGHT. What?

LEONORA. There was a lot you didn't tell me. . . .

DWIGHT. What are you getting at?

LEONORA. Do you know a man called Peter Walmsley?

DWIGHT. No.

LEONORA. Don't you?

DWIGHT. I don't think so. . . .
. . . Walmsley? Oh—not *Porky* Walmsley? . . . What about him?

LEONORA. Well, I've been spending the evening with him. He told me quite a lot about you.

DWIGHT. I hope he gave me a good character.

LEONORA. Terribly. . . . You seem to be rather a grand person, Steve.

DWIGHT. I guess, maybe, you're prejudiced.

LEONORA. Peter wasn't.

DWIGHT. Well, I'm certainly grateful to him.

LEONORA. It wasn't only him.

DWIGHT. What else?

.   .   .   .

LEONORA. I lay awake all last night wondering whether I hadn't been the world's biggest fool. I read Bertrand Russell to console me.

DWIGHT. And did he?

LEONORA. I found something that went right home to my midriff.

DWIGHT. Your—?

LEONORA. Midriff. He said: "Of all forms of caution, caution in love is perhaps the most fatal to true happiness." I howled when I read that.

DWIGHT. I wrote you the same thing last night.

LEONORA. You did?

DWIGHT. I was going to mail it from Cherbourg. (*With a smile.*) You thought you knew so much; that so long as you were in love with me, you couldn't know whether you liked me or not. I knew then that you'd never really been in love before. But I believed you'd come and find out if you liked me—later. Not so much later, either. When this cable came, I debated whether to see you or not.

LEONORA. You didn't!

DWIGHT. I thought it might be better for you to find out by yourself. Only—when life deliberately offers you a second chance, it seems ungrateful not to take it. It doesn't do it very often.

LEONORA. No.

DWIGHT. I hadn't reckoned on Porky! I think we're being rather spoiled.

LEONORA. So do I. (*She goes to him.*) I adore being spoiled. (*They start an embrace, and the telephone rings. They jump apart.*) At this time of night! (*She goes over to it.*) Hello? Hello?— ... *Who* wants me?—Vichy? (*Holds on.*) Good Lord! Mother and father. I hope there's nothing wrong. I'm afraid I'd forgotten all about them. (*Into*

phone.) Hello!—Yes— Yes— All right. (*Holds on again.*)
Hello! Hello, mother— Yes— (DWIGHT *seats himself just
behind her.*) No, darling. It's all right. I hadn't gone to
bed— No— I'm all right, mother— Why? Who told you
[I was sick?] Aunt Emily?—Oh, did she write to you?—
Oh! I'm sorry you've been worried, darling. But it wasn't
anything—really it wasn't. I was just putting her off.—Yes,
I know. It was naughty of me. And making you ring up
like this in the middle of the night.—You only just got her
letter?—I *am* sorry! Oh, I've been to the theatre, darling.
—Peter.—No, he's gone.—Yes, darling.—Yes, darling. (*She
listens as though to a long speech, and sits on* DWIGHT'S
knee.) Oh, darling I *am* sorry.—But you needn't do that.
I'm quite all right—really I am.—Oh, well, in that case—
When will you be back? Friday? The 15th? That's *this*
Friday!

DWIGHT. (*Sharply.*) You've got to sail Saturday!

LEONORA. Shut up. (*Into telephone.*) Well, darling, I've
rather a surprise for you. I think I'm going to be married
—no, darling—married—*married.*—No, of course it's not
Peter.—It's an American—it's rather nice, really.— (DWIGHT
kisses the back of her neck.) Don't do that! (*Back to
telephone.*) Nothing, mother—only it's here now, I—I—
(*She begins to giggle.*) I think you'd better speak to it!
Wait a minute. (*She hands the telephone to* DWIGHT.) Here!

DWIGHT. No!

LEONORA. Go on.

DWIGHT. Oh, well.—(*Taking telephone: tentatively speaking.*) Hello.—Mother?—

(LEONORA *lets out a peal of laughter.*)

THE IMPORTANCE OF BEING EARNEST [1]

by

Oscar Wilde

ERNEST *and* GWENDOLINE *are engaged. However,* GWENDO-
LINE'S *mother,* LADY BRACKNELL, *insists on looking after her
child's best interests. Here, she interviews* EARNEST.

LADY BRACKNELL. (*Enters left.*) Mr. Worthing! . . . [Be-
lieve me, sir,] . . . you are not engaged. . . . An engagement should always come on a young girl as a surprise,
pleasant or unpleasant, as the case may be. It is hardly a
matter that [Gwendoline] should be allowed to arrange for
herself. And now I have a few questions to put to you, Mr.
Worthing. . . . (*Sitting down left center.*) You can take a
seat, Mr. Worthing. (*Looks in her pocket for notebook and
pencil.*)

JACK. Thank you, Lady Bracknell. I prefer standing. . . .

LADY BRACKNELL. (*Pencil and notebook in hand.*) I feel
bound to tell you that you are not *down* on my list of
eligible young men; although I have the same list as the
dear Duchess of Bolton has. We work together, in fact.
However, I am quite ready to enter your name, should your
answers be what a really affectionate mother requires. Do
you smoke?

JACK. Well, yes, I must admit I smoke.

LADY BRACKNELL. I am glad to hear it. A man should always
have an occupation of some kind. There are far too many
idle men in London as it is. How *old* are you?

JACK. Thirty-five.

LADY BRACKNELL. A very good age to be married at. I have

always been of opinion that a man who desires to get married should either know everything or nothing. Which do you know?

JACK. I know nothing, Lady Bracknell. . . .

LADY BRACKNELL. I am pleased to hear it. I do not approve of anything that tampers with natural ignorance. Ignorance is like a delicate, exotic fruit; touch it and the bloom has gone. What is your income?

JACK. Between seven and eight thousand a year.

LADY BRACKNELL. (*Makes a note in her book.*) In land or in investments?

JACK. In investments, chiefly. (*Sitting sofa right center.*)

LADY BRACKNELL. That is satisfactory. What between the duties expected of one during one's lifetime and the duties exacted from one after one's death, land has ceased to be either a profit or a pleasure. It gives one position and prevents one from keeping it up. That's all that can be said about land.

JACK. I have a country house, with some land, of course, attached to it; about fifteen hundred acres, I believe, but I don't depend on that for my real income. As far as I can see, the poachers are the only people who make anything out of it.

LADY BRACKNELL. A country house? How many bedrooms? Well that point can be cleared up afterwards. (*Makes note.*) You have a *town* house, I hope? A girl with a simple unspoiled nature like Gwendoline could hardly be expected to reside in the country.

JACK. Well, I own a house in Belgrave Square, but it is let by the year to Lady Bloxham. Of course I can get it back whenever I like, at six months' notice.

LADY BRACKNELL. (*Severely.*) Lady Bloxham? I don't know her.

JACK. Oh, she goes about very little. She's a lady considerably advanced in years.

LADY BRACKNELL. Ah, nowadays that is no guarantee of respectability of character. What number in Belgrave Square?

JACK. One hundred and forty-nine.

LADY BRACKNELL. (*Closing pocket-book.*) The unfashionable side. I thought there was something! However, that could easily be altered. Now to minor matters. Are your parents living? (*Turning to* JACK.)

JACK. I have lost both my parents.

LADY BRACKNELL. Both? To lose one parent may be regarded as a misfortune—to lose both seems like carelessness. Who was your father? He seems to have been a man of wealth. Was he born in what the Radical papers call the purple of commerce, or did he rise from the ranks of the aristocracy?

JACK. I am afraid I really don't know. The fact is, Lady Bracknell, I said I had lost my parents. It would be nearer the truth to say that my parents seem to have lost me—I don't actually know who I am, by birth. I was—well—I was found. (*Rises.*)

LADY BRACKNELL. Found!

JACK. The late Mr. Thomas Cardew, an old gentleman of a very charitable and kindly disposition, found me, and gave me the name of Worthing, because he happened to have a first-class ticket for Worthing in his pocket at the time.

LADY BRACKNELL. *Where* did the charitable gentleman who had a first-class ticket for Worthing find you?

JACK. (*Gravely.*) In a handbag.

LADY BRACKNELL. A handbag!

JACK. (*Very seriously.*) Yes, Lady Bracknell. I was in a handbag—a somewhat large leather handbag, with handles to it—an ordinary handbag, in fact.

LADY BRACKNELL. In what locality did this Mr. Thomas Cardew come across this ordinary handbag?

JACK. In the cloakroom at Victoria Station. It was given him in mistake for his own.

LADY BRACKNELL. (*Rising.*) Mr. Worthing, I confess I feel somewhat bewildered by what you have just told me. To be born, or at any rate, bred, in a handbag, whether it had handles or not, seems to me to display a contempt for the ordinary decencies of family life that remind one of the worst excesses of the French Revolution—and I presume you know what that unfortunate movement led to? As for the particular locality in which the handbag was found, a cloakroom at a railway station might serve to conceal a social indiscretion—has probably, indeed, been used for that purpose before now—but it can hardly be regarded as an assured basis for a recognized position in good society.

JACK. May I ask you then what you would advise me to do? I need hardly say I would do anything in the world to insure Gwendoline's happiness.

LADY BRACKNELL. I would strongly advise you, Mr. Worthing, to try and acquire some relations as soon as possible, and to make a definite effort to produce, at any rate, one parent, of either sex, before the season is quite over. . . . Good morning, Mr. Worthing. (*Exits right.*)

JACK. Good morning. . . .

ROMEO AND JULIET

by

WILLIAM SHAKESPEARE

JULIET, *on her balcony, muses on her love for* ROMEO, *not knowing that he has braved her family's wrath by entering her garden.*

(JULIET *appears on the Balcony, and sits down.*)

[ROMEO]. But soft! What light through yonder window
 breaks!
It is the east, and Juliet is the sun!
Arise, fair sun, and kill the envious moon,
Who is already sick and pale with grief,
That thou, her maid, art far more fair than she.—
"It is my lady; Oh! it is my love:
"Oh, that she knew she were!"—
She speaks, yet she says nothing: what of that?
Her eye discourses: I will answer it.—
I am too bold.—Oh, were those eyes in heaven,
They would through the airy region stream so bright,
That birds would sing, and think it were the morn.—
See, how she leans her cheek upon her hand!
Oh, that I were a glove upon that hand,
That I might touch that cheek!

JULIET. Ah, me!

ROMEO. She speaks, she speaks!
Oh, speak again, bright angel! for thou art
As glorious to this sight, being o'er my head,
As is a wingèd messenger of heaven
To the up-turned wond'ring eyes of mortals,
When he bestrides the lazy-pacing clouds,
And sails upon the bosom of the air.

JULIET. Oh, Romeo, Romeo! wherefore art thou Romeo?
Deny thy father, and refuse thy name:
Or, if thou wilt not, be but sworn my love,
And I'll no longer be a Capulet.

ROMEO. Shall I hear more, or shall I speak at this?

JULIET. 'Tis but thy name that is my enemy!—
What's in a name? That which we call a rose,
By any other name would smell as sweet;
So Romeo would, were he not Romeo called,

Retain that dear perfection which he owes
Without that title!—Romeo, quit thy name;
And for that name, which is no part of thee,
Take all myself.

ROMEO. I take thee at thy word!   (JULIET *starts up*.)
Call me but love, I will forswear my name
And never more be Romeo.

JULIET. What man art thou, that, thus bescreened in night
So stumblest on my counsel?

ROMEO. I know not how to tell thee who I am!
My name, dear saint, is hateful to myself,
Because it is an enemy to thee.

JULIET. My ears have not yet drunk a hundred words
Of that tongue's uttering, yet I know the sound!
Art thou not Romeo, and a Montague?

ROMEO. Neither, fair saint, if either thee displease.

JULIET. How cam'st thou hither?—tell me—and for what?
The orchard walls are high, and hard to climb;
And the place, death,—considering who thou art,
If any of my kinsmen find thee here.

ROMEO. With love's light wings did I o'er-perch these walls;
For stony limits cannot hold love out;
And what love can do, that dares love attempt;
Therefore thy kinsmen are no stop to me.

JULIET. If they do see thee here, they'll murder thee.

ROMEO. Alack, there lies more peril in thine eye,
Than twenty of their swords! look thou but sweet,
And I am proof against their enmity.

JULIET. I would not, for the world, they saw thee here.
By whose direction found'st thou out this place?

ROMEO. By love, who first did prompt me to inquire;
He lent me counsel, and I lent him eyes.

I am no pilot; yet, wert thou as far
As that vast shore washed with the furthest sea,
I would adventure for such merchandise.

JULIET. Thou know'st, the mask of night is on my face,
Else would a maiden blush bepaint my cheek,
For that which thou hast heard me speak to-night.
Fain would I dwell on form; fain, fain deny
What I have spoke!—But farewell compliment!
Dost thou love me? I know thou wilt say—Ay;
And I will take thy word! yet, if thou swear'st,
Thou may'st prove false; at lovers' perjuries,
They say, Jove laughs. Oh, gentle Romeo,
If thou dost love, pronounce it faithfully!
Or, if thou think'st I am too quickly won,
I'll frown, and be perverse, and say thee nay,
So thou wilt woo! but else, not for the world.
In truth, fair Montague, I am too fond:
And therefore thou may'st think my 'haviour light!
But trust me, gentleman, I'll prove more true
Than those that have more cunning to be strange.
I should have been more strange, I must confess,
But that thou overheard'st, ere I was 'ware,
My true love's passion; therefore, pardon me,
And not impute this yielding to light love,
Which the dark night has so discovered.

ROMEO. Lady, by yonder blessèd moon I vow—

JULIET. Oh! swear not by the moon, the inconstant moon
That monthly changes in her circled orb;
Lest that thy love prove likewise variable.

ROMEO. What shall I swear by?

JULIET. Do not swear at all;
Or, if thou wilt, swear by thy gracious self
Which is the god of my idolatry,
And I'll believe thee.

ROMEO. If my true heart's love—

JULIET. Well, do not swear! Although I joy in thee,
I have no joy of this contract to-night;
It is too rash, too unadvised, too sudden,
Too like the lightning, which doth cease to be,
Ere one can say—It lightens. Sweet, good night!
This bud of love, by summer's ripening breath,
May prove a beauteous flower when next we meet.
Good night, good night!—as sweet repose and rest
Come to thy heart, as that within my breast!

ROMEO. Oh, wilt thou leave me so unsatisfied?

JULIET. What satisfaction canst thou have to-night?

ROMEO. The exchange of thy love's faithful vow for mine.

JULIET. I gave thee mine, before thou didst request it:
And yet I would it were to give again.

ROMEO. Would'st thou withdraw it? for what purpose, love?

JULIET. But to be frank, and give it thee again.
My bounty is as boundless as the sea,
My love as deep; the more I give to thee,
The more I have; for both are infinite.—
I hear some noise within.—Dear love, adieu!

FOR TWO MEN

GOODBYE AGAIN [1]

by

George Haight and Allan Scott

KENNETH BIXBY, *a lecturer, has been pursued by a girl, now married, whom he once knew. Her brother-in-law,* ARTHUR WESTLAKE, *has been delegated to settle the divorce of herself and her husband,* HARVEY WILSON. *As the scene opens,* KEN, (*who has no desire to marry* MRS. WILSON *should she be divorced*) *is in bed still, being the very gay master of a situation which he refuses to take seriously.* (*During the scene* KEN *addresses his secretary,* ANNE ROGERS).

KEN. . . . (*He . . . begins a quiet game of solitaire.*) Now I'm going to play Canfield. (*There is a knock at the door. As he plays, gaily.*) Come in.

(ARTHUR *enters with a briefcase.*)

ARTHUR. Oh—under the weather?

KEN. Certainly not!

ARTHUR. Good morning, Miss Rogers. . . . (*To* KEN.) Just getting up?

KEN. (*Playing solitaire carefully.*) Oh no.

ARTHUR. Aren't you going to—ah—ah—

KEN. No.

ARTHUR. Well, really—I—I—thought we all agreed on 10:30.

KEN. It's not 10: 30 yet.

ARTHUR. Well, I came here early purposely.

KEN. (*To* ANNE.) Ha ha! What did I tell you?

ARTHUR. Maybe you'd rather I gave you a few more moments—

KEN. Oh, no—come in, my good man—sit down—

ARTHUR. Well—to put it bluntly: aren't you going to get up?

KEN. Bluntly, no.

ARTHUR. Oh. (*He goes to the large chair and opens his briefcase.*)

KEN. Whatcha got in the bag? (ARTHUR *starts to answer.*) Papers? (ARTHUR *produces a sheaf.*) Legal papers? Where'd you get them?

ARTHUR. I've been up the whole night—but that's all right. I have endeavored to treat the case impartially and all parties concerned with fairness.

KEN. I've forgotten for the moment—did I retain you or did Mr. Wilson?

ARTHUR. Mr. Wilson—but that doesn't make any difference.

KEN. Would it make any difference if I retained you?

ARTHUR. Of course, in as much as—

KEN. Then I retain you.

ARTHUR. But that isn't what I meant.

KEN. What do you mean?

ARTHUR. (*All twisted.*) I don't know.—I've been up all night and I'm a little tired—but here it is in black and white. (*Handing the papers to* KEN.) What do you think of it?

KEN. You might try *Scribners*.

ARTHUR. I beg your pardon.

KEN. (*Reading.*) *Wilson vs. Wilson*—good title.

ARTHUR. When you're quite ready, Mr. Bixby, I should appreciate it if—

(*The telephone rings.* KEN *answers it.*)

KEN. Yes? All right. (KEN *relaxes, waiting.*)

ARTHUR. The duplicates are—

KEN. Sh! New York calling!

(*He listens intently and then quickly hangs up. He looks at watch, then the clock, gives the minute hand a tiny adjustment. He looks up brightly.*)

ARTHUR. I've marked in pencil lightly where you sign.

KEN. (*Interested.*) Where?

ARTHUR. Right there. And there. Your full name, of course.

KEN. (*Holds papers out to* ANNE.) Miss Rogers, will you sign these for me?

ARTHUR. Oh, no. They require your personal signature.

KEN. Oh, that's all right. Miss Rogers signs all my personal mail. Don't you, Miss Rogers?

ARTHUR. I'm afraid that won't do—these are documents.

KEN. I never sign my name—except on books and sometimes photographs. I'd be glad to do that for you.

ARTHUR. Mr. Bixby!

(*Telephone rings.* KEN *answers.*)

KEN. Hello? Oh—who? From— Oh yes, Mr. *Clayton.* By all means. Come right up. (*He hangs up.*) Miss Rogers— Mr. Clayton has not failed me. He is on his way up.

ARTHUR. (*Looking at his watch.*) I hope nothing will interfere with our 10:30 appointment.

KEN. (*Gaily.*) I'll be here. (*Shuffles deck and begins to play solitaire.*)

ARTHUR. Will you or will you not sign these papers?

KEN. (*Confidentially.*) You think I should?

ARTHUR. It will expedite matters—and do away with the necessity of an open scandal. Technically, it's an irregular procedure but since I hope to be a member of the family more or less and moreover since even a whisper of scandal would seriously endanger Mr. Wilson's business—I feel justified in taking these precautionary measures.

KEN. (*Busy with his game.*) Miss Rogers, I believe these cards are marked!

ARTHUR. (*Forcing pen and papers on* KEN.) I don't want to rush you— (KEN *plays solitaire.*) I would appreciate your attention!

KEN. You're a nuisance, *Arthur.*

ARTHUR. Since Miss Rogers is present I prefer to be a gentleman.

KEN. (*To* ANNE—*playing on.*) Nice having you here, Miss Rogers. (*Quiet knock on door.*) Come in! . . . Oh, Mr. Clayton, come right in. How do you do? . . .

THE SCHOOL FOR SCANDAL

by

RICHARD BRINSLEY SHERIDAN

CHARLES SURFACE, *an impecunious but good hearted young man is expecting financial aid from an* UNCLE OLIVER *who has just returned from foreign parts where he resided many years. In order to meet* CHARLES *incognito,* UNCLE OLIVER *poses as a broker, or money-lender, and offers to buy the family portraits from* CHARLES. *Young* CHARLES *proceeds with the business in rare good humor.*

CHARLES SURFACE. Walk in, gentlemen; pray walk in—here they are, the family of the Surfaces, up to the conquest.

SIR OLIVER. And, in my opinion, a goodly collection.

CHARLES SURFACE. Ay, ay, these are done in the true spirit of portrait-painting;—no *volontier grace* or expression. Not like the works of your modern Raphaels, who give you the strongest resemblance, yet contrive to make your portrait independent of you; so that you may sink the original, and not hurt the picture. No, no; the merit of these is the inveterate likeness—all stiff and awkward as the originals, and like nothing in human nature besides.

SIR OLIVER. Ah! we shall never see such figures of men again.

CHARLES SURFACE. I hope not.—Well, you see, Master Premium, what a domestic character I am: here I sit of an evening surrounded by my family.— . . . Egad, that's true; what's an auctioneer without his hammer? (*Taking pedigree down from right first wall.*) What parchment have we here?—O, our genealogy in full . . . here's the family tree . . . —this shall be [a] hammer, and now you may knock down my ancestors with their own pedigree.

SIR OLIVER. What an unnatural rogue!—an *ex post facto* parricide! . . .

CHARLES SURFACE. . . . —Well, here's my great uncle, Sir Richard Raveline, a marvellous good general in his day, I assure you. He served in all the Duke of Marlborough's wars, and got that cut over his eye at the battle of Malplaquet.—What say you, Mr. Premium?—look at him—there's a hero, not cut out of his feathers, as your modern clipt captains are, but enveloped in wig and regimentals, as a general should be.—What do you bid? . . . Why, then, [you] shall have him for ten pounds, and I'm sure that's not dear for a staff-officer.

SIR OLIVER. Heaven deliver me! his famous uncle Richard for ten pounds! (*Aside.*)—Very well, sir, I take him at that.

CHARLES SURFACE. . . . Knock down my uncle Richard.— Here, now, is a maiden sister of his, my great aunt Deborah, done by Kneller in his best manner, and esteemed a very formidable likeness.—There she is, you see, a shepherdess feeding her flock.—You shall have her for five pounds ten— the sheep are worth the money.

SIR OLIVER. Ah! poor Deborah! a woman who set such a value on herself! (*Aside.*)—Five pounds ten—she's mine.

CHARLES SURFACE. Knock down my aunt Deborah. . . . This, now, is a grandfather of my mother's, a learned judge, well known on the western circuit.—What do you rate him at, . . . ?

SIR OLIVER. Four guineas.

CHARLES SURFACE. Four guineas!—Gad's life, you don't bid me the price of his wig.—Mr. Premium, you have more respect for the woolsack; do let us knock his lordship down at fifteen.

SIR OLIVER. By all means.

CHARLES SURFACE. And there are two brothers of his, William and Walter Blunt, Esquires, both members of parliament and noted speakers; and what's very extraordinary, I believe, this is the first time they were ever bought or sold.

SIR OLIVER. That is very extraordinary, indeed! I'll take them at your own price, for the honour of parliament.

[CHARLES] Well said, little Premium!—I'll knock them down at forty. . . . Here's a jolly fellow—I don't know what relation, but he was mayor of Norwich: take him at eight pounds.

SIR OLIVER. No, no: six will do for the mayor.

CHARLES SURFACE. Come, make it guineas, and I throw the two aldermen there into the bargain.

SIR OLIVER. They're mine.

CHARLES SURFACE. . . . Knock down the mayor and aldermen.—But, plague on't, we shall be all day retailing in this manner; do let us deal wholesale: what say you, little Premium? Give me three hundred pounds, and take all that remains on each side in a lump. . . .

SIR OLIVER. Well, well, any thing to accommodate you so they are mine. But there is one portrait which you have always passed over.

[CHARLES.] (*Having put the chair away comes forward, left.*) What, that ill-looking little fellow over the settee?

SIR OLIVER. Yes, yes, I mean that, though I don't think him so ill-looking a little fellow, by any means.

CHARLES SURFACE. What, that?—Oh! that's my uncle Oliver; 'twas done before he went to India. . . .

SIR OLIVER. . . . I think it as honest a looking face as any in the room, dead or alive;—but I suppose uncle Oliver goes with the rest of the lumber?

CHARLES SURFACE. No, hang it; I'll not part with poor Noll. The old fellow has been very good to me, and, egad, I'll keep his picture while I've a room to put it in.

SIR OLIVER. The rogue's my nephew after all! (*Aside.*)— But, sir, I have somehow taken a fancy to that picture.

CHARLES SURFACE. I'm sorry for't, for you certainly will not have it.—Oons, haven't you got enough of them?

SIR OLIVER. I forgive him every thing! (*Aside.*)—But, sir,

when I take a whim in my head I don't value money. I'll give you as much for that as for all the rest.

CHARLES SURFACE. Don't tease me, master broker; I tell you I'll not part with it, and there's an end of it.

SIR OLIVER. How like his father the dog is! (*Aside.*)—Well, well, I have done.—I did not perceive it before, but I think I never saw such a resemblance—(*Aside.*)—Here is a draft for your sum. (*Taking it out of his pocket book.*)

CHARLES SURFACE. Why, 'tis for eight hundred pounds.

SIR OLIVER. You will not let Sir Oliver go?

CHARLES SURFACE. Zounds! no!—I tell you once more.

SIR OLIVER. Then never mind the difference, we'll balance that another time—but give your hand on the bargain, you are an honest fellow, Charles—I beg your pardon, sir, for being so free.—Come, [I must go.] . . .

THE MERCHANT GENTLEMAN [1]

by

MOLIÈRE
Translated by Margaret Baker

M. JOURDAIN, *a nouveau-riche, has so great a desire for culture that he assembles masters of fencing, dancing, music, and philosophy. The last gentleman engages in a vigorous argument with the others over the value of his subject, and a free-for-all is barely averted. After this* M. JOURDAIN *begins his lesson with the* MASTER OF PHILOSOPHY.

M. JOURDAIN. Oh! beat each other as much as you please. I can't help it, and I am not going to spoil my robe to separate you. I should indeed be a fool to thrust myself among you and catch a blow that would hurt me.

(*Re-enter* MASTER OF PHILOSOPHY, *arranging his collar.*) . . .

MASTER OF PHILOSOPHY. Come, your lesson.

M. JOURDAIN. Ah, my dear Monsieur, I am sorry you have been so maltreated.

MASTER OF PHILOSOPHY. That is of no consequence. A philosopher knows how to accept such things in a proper spirit. . . . But never mind that; what is it you wish to learn?

M. JOURDAIN. All that I can, for I have every desire in the world to become learned; I am incensed that my father and mother did not make me study all the sciences when I was young.

MASTER OF PHILOSOPHY. That sentiment is reasonable, *Nam, sine doctrina, vita est quasi mortis imago.* You understand that,—you know Latin, of course?

M. JOURDAIN. Yes, but imagine that I don't. Tell me what the words mean.

MASTER OF PHILOSOPHY. They mean: "Without science, life is almost an image of death."

M. JOURDAIN. The Latin is right.

MASTER OF PHILOSOPHY. Have you not some principles, some foundation or beginnings of the sciences?

M. JOURDAIN. (*With great satisfaction.*) Oh! yes, I can read and write.

MASTER OF PHILOSOPHY. Where do you wish to begin? Would you like to have me teach you logic?

M. JOURDAIN. Logic? What is logic?

MASTER OF PHILOSOPHY. Logic teaches the three operations of the mind.

M. JOURDAIN. And what are the three operations of the mind?

MASTER OF PHILOSOPHY. The first, the second and the third. (*Pause.*) The first is to conceive by means of the universal; the second is to judge by means of categories; and the third is to draw conclusions by means of the syllogism—*Celarent, Darii, Ferio, Baralipton, Barbara,* etc.

M. JOURDAIN. These words are too barbarous. Logic doesn't suit me. Let us learn something else that's pleasanter.

MASTER OF PHILOSOPHY. Would you like to learn ethics?

M. JOURDAIN. Ethics?

MASTER OF PHILOSOPHY. Yes.

M. JOURDAIN. What is Ethics?

MASTER OF PHILOSOPHY. It treats of happiness, teaches men to moderate their passions and——

M. JOURDAIN. No, not that. I am passionate and irascible as all the devils, and that would be of no use. I want to fly into a rage as often as I like.

MASTER OF PHILOSOPHY. Perhaps you would like to learn Physics?

M. JOURDAIN. What is Physics?

MASTER OF PHILOSOPHY. Physics is the science which explains the principles of all natural phenomena and the properties of bodies; which treats of the nature of the elements, of metals and minerals, rocks, plants and animals, and teaches us the causes of all the meteors, the rainbow, lightning, thunder, rain, snow, hail, winds and tornadoes.

M. JOURDAIN. There is too much hurly-burly about that: too much confusion.

MASTER OF PHILOSOPHY. What, then, would you have me teach you?

M. JOURDAIN. (*Leaning eagerly toward the Philosopher.*) Will you teach me orthography?

MASTER OF PHILOSOPHY. Very willingly.

M. JOURDAIN. Afterwards you may teach me the almanac; so that I may know when there is a moon, and when not.

MASTER OF PHILOSOPHY. Very well. In order to follow your thoughts and treat the subject in a philosophical way, it is necessary to begin according to the order of things. . . . I shall explain all these peculiarities in detail.

M. JOURDAIN. I pray you, do. And now I must tell you a secret. I am in love with a woman of quality, and I want you to help me write her a little note which I shall drop at her feet.

MASTER OF PHILOSOPHY. Very well.

M. JOURDAIN. It will be gallant, will it not?

MASTER OF PHILOSOPHY. Without a doubt. Do you wish to write a poem to her?

M. JOURDAIN. No, no, no; not poetry!

MASTER OF PHILOSOPHY. You are only going to write prose?

M. JOURDAIN. No, I don't want prose—and I don't want poetry.

MASTER OF PHILOSOPHY. It must be one or the other.

M. JOURDAIN. Why?

MASTER OF PHILOSOPHY. For the simple reason, Monsieur, that there is no way to express one's self except in poetry or prose.

M. JOURDAIN. There is nothing but prose and poetry?

MASTER OF PHILOSOPHY. Nothing. All that is not prose is poetry, and all that is not poetry is prose.

M. JOURDAIN. And when one speaks, what is that?

MASTER OF PHILOSOPHY. That is prose.

M. JOURDAIN. What! when I say, "Nicole, bring me my slippers and give me my night-cap," is that prose?

MASTER OF PHILOSOPHY. Yes, Monsieur.

M. JOURDAIN. By my faith, I have spoken prose for more than forty years without knowing it! I am greatly obliged to you for teaching me this. I should like, then, to say in the letter: "Beautiful Marquise, your beautiful eyes make me to die of love;" but I want it expressed in a gallant manner, I wish to have the sentence well turned.

MASTER OF PHILOSOPHY. Write: "The fires of your eyes reduce my heart to cinders; I suffer night and day with the intensity of a——"

M. JOURDAIN. No, no, no, I don't want all that; I want only what I have told you; "Beautiful Marquise, your beautiful eyes make me to die of love."

MASTER OF PHILOSOPHY. It would be well to embellish this a little.

M. JOURDAIN. No, I tell you, I wish only these words in the note; but prettily turned, arranged in the best possible way. I beg you to repeat them to me in various ways so that I may hear how they sound.

MASTER OF PHILOSOPHY. One could say first: "Beautiful marquise, your beautiful eyes make me to die of love." Or "Of love die, make me, beautiful marquise, your beautiful eyes." Or "Your eyes beautiful with love make me, beautiful marquise, die." Or again: "Die, your beautiful eyes, beautiful marquise, of love me make."

M. JOURDAIN. But of all these ways, which is the best?

MASTER OF PHILOSOPHY. Your way: "Beautiful marquise, your beautiful eyes make me to die of love."

M. JOURDAIN. And yet I have never studied, and I did that

the first stroke! I thank you with all my heart, and I pray
you come early to-morrow.

JULIUS CAESAR

by

William Shakespeare

BRUTUS *and* CASSIUS, *long fast friends, have a difference of
opinions.*

CASSIUS. That you have wronged me doth appear in this:
You have condemned and noted Lucius Pella,
For taking bribes here of the Sardians;
Wherein, my letters, praying on his side,
Because I knew the man, were slighted off.

BRUTUS. You wronged yourself to write in such a case.

CASSIUS. In such a time as this, it is not meet
That every nice offence should bear his comment.

BRUTUS. Let me tell you, Cassius, you yourself
Are much condemned to have an itching palm;
To sell and mart your offices for gold
To undeservers.

CASSIUS. I, an itching palm!—
You know that you are Brutus that speak this,
Or, by the gods, this speech were else your last.

BRUTUS. Remember March—the ides of March remember;
Did not great Julius bleed for justice' sake?
What villain touched his body, that did stab,
And not for justice? What, shall one of us,
That struck the foremost man of all this world,
But for supporting robbers—shall we now
Contaminate our fingers with base bribes,

And sell the mighty space of our large honors
For so much trash, as may be grasped thus?
I had rather be a dog, and bay the moon,
Than such a Roman.

CASSIUS. Brutus, bay not me;
I'll not endure it: I am a soldier, I,
Older in practice, abler than yourself
To make conditions.

BRUTUS. Go to; you're not Cassius.

CASSIUS. I am.

BRUTUS. I say, you are not.

CASSIUS. Urge me no more: I shall forget myself:
Have mind upon your health, tempt me no further.

BRUTUS. Away, slight man!

CASSIUS. Is't possible?—

BRUTUS. Hear me, for I will speak.—
Must I give way and room to your rash choler?
Shall I be frighted, when a madman stares?

CASSIUS. Ye gods! ye gods! Must I endure all this?

BRUTUS. (*Nearer.*) All this? ay, more!—Fret till your proud
    heart break.—
Go, show your slaves how choleric you are,
And make your bondmen tremble: Must I budge?
Must I observe you? Must I stand and crouch
Under your testy humor?—by the gods
You shall digest the venom of your spleen,
Though it do split you; for, from this day forth,
I'll use you for my mirth—yea, for my laughter—
When you are waspish.

CASSIUS. Is it come to this?

BRUTUS. You say, you are a better soldier:
Let it appear so; make your vaunting true,

And it shall please me well: for mine own part,
I shall be glad to learn of noble men.

CASSIUS. You wrong me, every way you wrong me, Brutus.
I said, an elder soldier, not a better:
Did I say better?

BRUTUS. If you did, I care not.

CASSIUS. When Cæsar lived, he durst not thus have moved me.

BRUTUS. Peace, peace; you durst not so have tempted him.

CASSIUS. I durst not?

BRUTUS. No.

CASSIUS. What? durst not tempt him?

BRUTUS. For your life, you durst not.

CASSIUS. Do not presume too much upon my love;
I may do that I shall be sorry for.

BRUTUS. You have done that you should be sorry for.
There is no terror, Cassius, in your threats;
For I am armed so strong in honesty,
That they pass by me as the idle wind
Which I respect not. I did send to you
For certain sums of gold, which you denied me;
For I can raise no money by vile means;
By heaven, I had rather coin my heart,
And drop my blood for drachmas, than to wring
From the hard hands of peasants their vile trash,
By any indirection. I did send
To you for gold to pay my legions,
Which you denied me: Was that done like Cassius?
Should I have answered Caius Cassius so?
When Marcus Brutus grows so covetous,
To lock such rascal counters from his friends
Be ready, gods, with all your thunderbolts,
Dash him to pieces!

CASSIUS. I denied you not.

BRUTUS. You did.

CASSIUS. I did not:—He was but a fool
That brought my answer back.—Brutus hath rived my
  heart:
A friend should bear his friend's infirmities;
But Brutus makes mine greater than they are.

BRUTUS. I do not, till you practice them on me.

CASSIUS. You love me not.

BRUTUS. I do not like your faults.

CASSIUS. A friendly eye could never see such faults.

BRUTUS. A flatterer's would not, though they do appear
As huge as high Olympus.

CASSIUS. Come, Antony, and, young Octavius, come,
Revenge yourselves alone on Cassius;
For Cassius is aweary of the world;
Hated by one he loves; braved by his brother;
Checked like a bondman: all his faults observed,
Set in a note-book, learned, and conned by rote,
To cast into my teeth. Oh, I could weep
My spirit from mine eyes!—There is my dagger,
And here my naked breast; within, a heart
Dearer than Plutus' mine, richer than gold:
If that thou be'st a Roman, take it forth;
I, that denied thee gold, will give my heart:
Strike, as thou didst at Cæsar: for, I know,
When thou didst hate him worst, thou lovedst him better
Than ever thou lov'dst Cassius.

BRUTUS. Sheathe your dagger;
Be angry when you will, it shall have scope;
Do what you will, dishonor shall be humor.
Oh, Cassius, you are yoked with a lamb

That carries anger, as the flint bears fire;
Who, much enforced, shows a hasty spark,
And straight is cold again.

CASSIUS. Hath Cassius lived
To be but mirth and laughter to his Brutus,
When grief, and blood ill-tempered, vexeth him?

BRUTUS. When I spoke that, I was ill-tempered too.

CASSIUS. Do you confess so much? Give me your hand.

BRUTUS. (*Both embrace, center.*) And my heart too.

CASSIUS. Oh, Brutus!—

BRUTUS. What's the matter?

CASSIUS. Have not you love enough to bear with me,
When that rash humor which my mother gave me,
Makes me forgetful?

BRUTUS. Yes, Cassius; and henceforth,
When you are over-earnest with your Brutus,
He'll think your mother chides, and leave you.

FOR TWO WOMEN

A CHURCH MOUSE [1]

by

LADISLAUS FODOR

OLLY, *once the Baron's secretary, then his mistress, then discarded, returns to see her successor as secretary,* SUSIE. *There is no love lost between them.* OLLY *has seen the Baron and made an evening appointment with him. She is still in the office when* SUSIE *enters.*

SUSIE. . . . So you're here . . . !

OLLY. . . . Yes, but no thanks to you. I've just had a delightful chat with your carefully guarded employer— What do you mean by trying to keep me from seeing him?

SUSIE. He's here on business. He has no time for women. (*Crosses; puts wrap on settee.*)

OLLY. No? Well, he seems to have time for me. He's just invited me to have supper with him.

SUSIE. (*Fearfully upset.*) Just invited— You're going out with the Baron tonight?

OLLY. Tonight! At nine. So your scheming went for nothing. It made me furious at first, but I really ought to thank you. You've been the greatest help to me.

SUSIE. Don't thank me. I had no desire to help you.

OLLY. (*In fine humor and amused by* SUSIE.) What a child

you are! Not to know that the moment a man is told he can't see a woman he lets nothing keep him from her. (*Sits at typewriter table.*) Tonight you turned *me* into a sort of forbidden fruit. You remember what happened to Adam. (*She flicks her cigarette ashes off on* SUSIE'S *typewriter table.*)

SUSIE. (*Crosses to below table; brushes ashes. Cold with rage.*) Please don't mess up my table.

OLLY. (*Laughing and crosses to table at settee to crush cigarette.*) Don't worry—I don't want your *typewriter*.

SUSIE. (*Confronts her.*) I know what you want—you want to come back to the bank.

OLLY. You're wrong again. The bank wants to come to me. It's amusing, my dear. You try to keep me from him, and instead, you throw me right into his arms.

SUSIE. How vulgar you are!

OLLY. (*Amused.*) Do you think it's vulgar to be in a man's arms? (*Sits left end settee.*) Haven't you ever longed to feel his arms around you?

SUSIE. (*Frantic with jealousy.*) You talk about a man like the Baron as if he were a clerk.

OLLY. Men are all alike when it comes to women.

SUSIE. Not your kind of women. He's not the kind of a man to care for a girl like you.

OLLY. No? What's the matter with *me?*

SUSIE. (*Scornfully.*) Why, you're nothing! Just beautiful—that's all!

OLLY. (*Rises.*) It's plenty! And since we are paying compliments—you're not bad looking yourself—and you have quite a decent figure—(*She looks* SUSIE *all over.*)—only you don't know what to do with it.

SUSIE. How do you mean?

OLLY. In perfecting yourself as a machine you've neglected yourself as a woman.

SUSIE. (*Center proudly.*) Baron told me I was the best secretary he ever had.

OLLY. Is that any consolation after working here—he leaves *you* to go out with *me?*

SUSIE. (*Crosses to chair center. Bewildered.*) What—what can he see in a person like you?

OLLY. He'd see the same thing in you if you took the trouble. He sees a woman who is warm and human—whose skin is soft and perfumed—a woman who—

SUSIE. I won't let you say that. He isn't that kind of man at all.

OLLY. (*Laughs delightfully.*) As if you knew what kind of a man he is! (*She crosses closer to* SUSIE *as she grows more interested.*) You have an idea he's all brain and business. You can't imagine him having a weakness. But I assure you—he was right down on my level tonight. Don't you think his fingers tingle when they touch mine? Do you suppose he doesn't grow dizzy when he inhales my perfume?

SUSIE. (*With regretful admission.*) He *did* remember your perfume.

OLLY. (*Warming to her subject,* OLLY *unmeaningly, puts many ideas in* SUSIE's *head.*) Don't you think his heart beats faster when I lean against him? By accident?

SUSIE. (*Absorbing all this.*) By accident?

OLLY. By intentional accident! And how men love it! It's like this—(*She explains, acting it out.*)—a quick movement—you touch him in one breath-taking second—you pull back—you say naively, "Oh, pardon me!" He murmurs something—

SUSIE. (*Like a child.*) I wonder.

OLLY. (*Paying no attention to this remark.*)—the air is charged with electricity—he struggles for his self-control—and just as he almost *has* it—

SUSIE. (*So absorbed she forgets everything else.*) Yes?

OLLY. —you start all over again! Then his arms begin to ache to hold you—they steal around you. And if you're a smart girl you say, "Oh, no! You mustn't!"

SUSIE. (*All ears.*) And then he stops?

OLLY. Stops? Of course he doesn't stop. He goes on. He pulls you closer—you struggle—but not much.

SUSIE. (*Struggling by herself.*) Eh—

OLLY. —he murmurs incoherently—

SUSIE. (*All eagerness.*) And what does he say?

OLLY. (*Is now living over a past love scene and is swept along with her thoughts.*) It doesn't matter! You don't care! His arms tighten! Your head begins to whirl! A delicious faintness sweeps over you! His eyes look into yours!

SUSIE. (*Dreamily.*) His eyes!

OLLY. (*Graphically.*) His lips come closer! You are limp! You resist no more! Your eye-lashes flutter down! You see him no longer! All you know is the wonderful strength of his embrace!

SUSIE. (*In a faint whisper.*) And then?

OLLY. He kisses you!

SUSIE. (*More faintly still.*) And then?

OLLY. And then—

SUSIE. How you tell it! I almost lived it!

OLLY. (*Takes cigarette; lights it. Contemptuously.*) You? You never will. You're a prude! If a man glimpsed you from a distance and thought "now there's a sweet spot to rest"—when he caught up with you he'd see "Keep-off-the-grass" signs hung all over you.

SUSIE. (*Haughtily.*) You know nothing about me. Well, I may look green but I'm not grass.

OLLY. You're just a well-oiled and regulated machine. You'll probably marry another machine and have a flock of little typewriters.

SUSIE. (*Crosses to typewriter chair, almost in tears she is so angry.*) Even that would be better than to be like you. All you think of is love-making.

OLLY. You forget that my business is other people's happiness.

SUSIE. (*Facing her defiantly.*) I suppose you've won—but it won't last. Even if you get him you can't hold him.

OLLY. Do you think *you* could?

SUSIE. (*Slowly.*) I've never tried and I wouldn't want to, like that.

OLLY. (*Highly entertained.*) Why don't you? It would probably amuse him.

SUSIE. (*Who has stood all she can.*) Didn't you say you were going to dress? *He* doesn't like to be kept waiting.

OLLY. (*Crosses up center.*) Don't worry—I'm not taking any chances. (*She crosses to center door. Turns for a parting shot.*) But don't waste your time playing vampire, dear. You're a fast typist, but as a siren I'm convinced you'd fail.

CHILDREN OF THE MOON [1]

by

MARTIN FLAVIN

LAURA ATHERTON, *a possessive mother, returns home from a trip abroad earlier than expected. She has heard from her daughter* JANE *that the girl is interested in a* MAJOR BANNISTER, *an aviator recuperating in the Atherton home after a crash on their grounds.* MRS. ATHERTON *has lost a son who had been an airman, in the war, and prides herself on* "living only for her remaining child." *She is greeted by the more mellow* MADAM ATHERTON (LAURA's *mother-in-law*) *who, out of sympathy for the young lovers, has not told them of* LAURA's *impending return.*

(LAURA *comes in at the door. . . .* LAURA *is a tall, slender, elegant woman, dressed very smartly in deep black. She has been beautiful and is still charming. Her face shows the marks of grief and anxiety, and is startlingly but becomingly colorless. She is quick and impetuous, almost staccato, in movement and speech. She submits to* MADAM ATHERTON's *embrace and responds to it, but without real warmth, and quickly disengages herself.*)

LAURA. And Jane? Where is Jane?

MADAM. (*Easily.*) She will be here directly.

LAURA. (*Bewildered.*). Oh! . . . Jane is ill?

MADAM. No, no, Laura, there is nothing amiss with Jane. . . . (*Taking her arm and going toward the couch.*) Come, my dear, sit down by the fire. You must be cold. . . .

LAURA. But Jane? Where is Jane?

MADAM. She is dressing for dinner.

[1] Copyright, 1924, by Martin Flavin.

LAURA. Dressing for dinner!

MADAM. (*With a note of exasperation.*) Well, she didn't expect you so soon, Laura.

LAURA. Oh! (*She suffers herself to be divested of her coat, and taking off her hat, sits down on the couch with a sigh of weariness.* MADAM ATHERTON *takes the hat and coat. . . .*)

MADAM. I expect you've had a tiresome trip.

LAURA. (*With a shudder.*) Ghastly!

MADAM. (*Sympathetically.*) Too bad, too bad.

LAURA. And ever since the train got in I have been in agony. . . . Just that. When I did not see Jane at the station, I was convinced that she was ill—seriously ill.

MADAM. Nonsense, my dear.

LAURA. Yes, but just think: I have never been away from home since Jane was old enough to walk that she has not met me on my return.

[MADAM.] (*Lightly.*) Well, there has to be a first time for everything, Laura.

LAURA. There should never be a first time for lack of consideration or respect for one's mother.

MADAM. (*Hastily.*) But William could have told you that she was perfectly well.

LAURA. He did. But he is such a stupid fellow, I—I didn't feel sure.

MADAM. I'm dreadfully sorry you've had all this needless anxiety.

LAURA. (*Petulantly.*) Yes, but I don't understand it now. Why wasn't Jane at the station?

MADAM. Oh! Well, you see, Laura, I didn't get your note until this morning. And Jane had some plans for the afternoon which I thought it would be unfortunate to disturb, so I didn't tell her.

LAURA. (*Incredulously.*) You didn't tell her? You didn't tell her that her mother was coming home?

MADAM. (*Shaking her head calmly.*) No.

LAURA. You mean to say she doesn't know it now?

MADAM. No.

LAURA. Well, that is quite the most extraordinary thing I ever heard of. What plans could the child have that would weigh against her mother's return?

MADAM. (*Placidly.*) Perhaps I made a mistake, Laura.

LAURA. Indeed you did, Mother Atherton; a great mistake. When I think of all that I have suffered in the last two hours—

MADAM. I am very sorry, my dear. . . .

LAURA. (*Theatrically.*) . . . You don't understand the relationship . . . between Jane and her mother. I have lived for my children, and since—(*Her voice quavers.*) since my great affliction, I have lived for my child. My whole existence is dedicated to my daughter. . . .

MADAM. (*Unimpressed.*) Yes, of course, my dear; but tell me: your note was such a complete surprise, why did you change your plans?

LAURA. Entirely on Jane's account.

MADAM. On Jane's account?

LAURA. Yes. She wrote me about the accident to this—this aviator.

MADAM. (*Suggesting politely.*) Major Bannister.

LAURA. Yes. I felt concerned about it; I hardly know why. Then she mentioned him again in another letter rather— rather too warmly.

MADAM. Yes?

LAURA. Of course, I know that Jane would never permit herself to become interested in an aviator.

[MADAM.] (*Innocently.*) But why not an aviator?

LAURA. Have you forgotten . . . that my son was an aviator and that he lost his life in the air? . . .

MADAM. Yes, my dear? You were saying?

LAURA. (*Dabbing at her eyes.*) I felt that she needed me; that is all. Needed the protection of a mother's arms; the watchfulness of a mother's eyes.

MADAM. (*Sighing.*) Yes, Laura, I quite understand.

LAURA. And so I gave up my trip. I cancelled my reservations and took the first train back. (*Proudly. . . .*) You see, I am an old-fashioned mother . . . I sacrifice everything for my child. . . . I suppose the man has gone? I could not, of course, condescend to question William.

MADAM. Naturally. (*After a pause.*) No, he has not gone, Laura.

LAURA. Oh! (*Exultantly.*) I am glad that I came back.

MADAM. Major Bannister and Jane had planned a picnic this afternoon at Neptune's Pool. That is why I did not tell her you were coming.

LAURA. (*Incredulously.*) And that is the plan you thought would be of more importance to her than her mother's return?

MADAM. I thought it would be a pity to disturb it.

LAURA. (*Contemptuously.*) Oh! How little you know her! And do you mean to say that you permit her to go about unchaperoned with this—this aviator?

MADAM. I think you may trust my judgment and discretion in such matters.

LAURA. It is fortunate indeed that I came home. I had a premonition of this.

[MADAM.] Major Bannister is a gentleman, Laura, a man of fine family, wealthy, distinguished. We know his antecedents thoroughly.

LAURA. Oh! And what has that to do with it? . . . It does not matter to me who or what he is. I disapprove of it utterly. And I am amazed at you, Mother Atherton, amazed at you for having permitted it.

MADAM. But Laura—

LAURA. Jane is a mere child.

MADAM. She is older than you were when you married my son.

LAURA. What has that to do with it?

MADAM. (*Gently.*) Nothing, perhaps. But I must beg you to consider that Jane is actually no longer a child, and has already reached an age when the engagement of her affections may not unreasonably be expected.

LAURA. (*Springing to her feet.*) You—you can't mean that she cares for this man?

MADAM. I know that she does.

LAURA. (*Through set teeth.*) If that is true, I shall never forgive you.

"THE PATSY" [1]

by

BARRY CONNERS

PAT, *the insignificant younger sister, seems unable ever to please her mother and older sister. Her father has just*

[1] Copyright, 1925, by Barry Conners (under the title "Love Lesson"). Copyright, 1927, by Samuel French.

taken her side, and evoked a quarrel thereby with his wife.
PAT *and* GRACE, *the older sister, speak.*

GRACE. Where's Father?

PATRICIA. He's gone.

GRACE. (*Pausing left of sofa and glaring at* PATRICIA.) Now
see what you've done. (PATRICIA *smiles at her.*) You've done
everything else you could—(*Puts wrap on sofa.*) now you've
separated your own father and mother!

PATRICIA. (*Looks at her coolly a moment.*) Some day somebody is going to sprinkle insect powder on you!

GRACE. You don't say so! . . .

PATRICIA. (*Notices wrap.*) Are you going to wear that wrap
of mine again?

GRACE. Yes, I am. I suppose you're going to start another
row about it.

PATRICIA. Nope. Go right ahead and wear it. I don't want it.
You can have it. It's yours. I make you a present of it.

GRACE. Thanks.

PATRICIA. You're welcome.

GRACE. . . . (*Smiles a nasty smile. Puts wrap back stage.*)
So you're not going to the dance after all, are you?

PATRICIA. Nope.

GRACE. I told you you weren't, didn't I?

PATRICIA. Yes.

GRACE. Maybe the next time you'll believe me!

PATRICIA. No, I won't. There isn't going to be any next time.

GRACE. Oh, isn't there?

PATRICIA. (*Quietly.*) Nope! I won't be here the next time.

You can have it all to yourself and do anything you like. (*Rise.*) There won't be anybody to interfere.

GRACE. (*Sarcastically.*) Oh, I suppose you're going to leave home now.

PATRICIA. (*Quietly.*) Yes. That's just what I'm going to do. (*Walk up and down.*) I make too much trouble in this place—somehow—and I got Ma and Pop fighting over me—(*She struggles to keep back tears.*) and I've never been anything but a curse to Ma ever since I was born—(*With some resentment showing through coming tears.*) and she never wanted me anyway— (*She puts the handkerchief to her eyes and turning her head away silently cries.*)

GRACE. (*Vindictively.*) You ought to cry! You ought to cry! And if I had the authority I'd give you something to cry for!

PATRICIA. (*Drops her hands and looks at her. She stares a moment, vengefully, and then, steadily glaring at her, slowly rises. She reaches her height and then slowly starts to move toward* GRACE *as though she intended tackling her.*) You would—would you? (*Crosses slowly.*)

GRACE. (*Who has maintained an attitude of fearless defiance, suddenly loses her nerve and runs, calling loudly.*) Mother! Mother! Mother!

PATRICIA. (*Frightened—instantly in a panic of whispered pleading to prevent more trouble.*) Grace! Please don't, will you? Please! I was only fooling! Please! . . . (*Pleadingly —whispers.*) Grace! (*She makes a frantic sign.* [*Grace quiets down.*] . . . *Very quietly.*) All right, Grace, all right. I was going to do the sportsmanlike thing to-night. But now I won't. As soon as you go I'm going to do you a dirty trick!

GRACE. What do you mean?

PATRICIA. (*Laughs in spite of herself. She pauses.*) I mean something about Tony Anderson.

GRACE. (*Smiles.*) What will you bet he . . . come[s] home with me to-night?

PATRICIA. I won't bet. You wouldn't pay a bet if you lost.

GRACE. Just the same I'll bet he comes home with me.

PATRICIA. Suppose he does. But that won't make any difference. If he comes home with you a hundred times—I'll take him away from you just the same. (*Crosses to door.*)

GRACE. (*Smiles.*) After to-night he won't as much as give you a pleasant look, you insignificant little gnat.

PATRICIA. No? All right. This is a case of mind over matter, dearie. I don't mind what you say—because you don't matter. . . .

LADY WINDERMERE'S FAN [1]

by

OSCAR WILDE

MRS. ERLYNNE, *knowing full well the dismal life of a fallen woman of the 1890's follows* LADY WINDERMERE *to a rendezvous at* LORD DARLINGTON'S *rooms, and begs* LADY WINDERMERE *to return to her husband before she makes a fatal misstep out of spite.*

LADY WINDERMERE. . . . Why doesn't he come? This waiting is horrible. He should be here. . . . Arthur must have read my letter by this time. If he cared for me, he would have come after me, would have taken me back by force. But he doesn't care. He's entrammeled by this woman—fascinated by her—dominated by her. If a woman wants to hold a man, she has merely to appeal to what is worst in him. We make gods of men, and they leave us. Others make

[1] Copyright, 1893, by Oscar Wilde.

brutes of them and they fawn and are faithful. How hideous life is!—Oh! it was mad of me to come here, horribly mad. And yet which is the worst, I wonder, to be at the mercy of a man who loves one, or the wife of a man who in one's own house dishonors one? What woman knows? What woman in the whole world? . . . No, no! I will go back, let Arthur do with me what he pleases. I can't wait here. It has been madness my coming. I must go at once. As for Lord Darlington— Oh! here he is! What shall I do? . . . (*Hides her face in her hands. Enter* MRS. ERLYNNE *left.*)

MRS. ERLYNNE. Lady Windermere! (LADY WINDERMERE *starts and looks up. Then recoils in contempt.*) Thank Heaven I am in time. You must go back to your husband's house immediately.

LADY WINDERMERE. Must?

MRS. ERLYNNE. (*Authoritatively.*) Yes, you must! There is not a second to be lost. Lord Darlington may return at any moment.

LADY WINDERMERE. Don't come near me!

MRS. ERLYNNE. Oh! you are on the brink of ruin; you are on the brink of a hideous precipice. You must leave this place at once, my carriage is waiting at the corner of the street. You must come with me and drive straight home. (LADY WINDERMERE *throws off her cloak and flings it on the sofa.*) What are you doing?

LADY WINDERMERE. Mrs. Erlynne—if you had not come here, I would have gone back. But now that I see you, I feel that nothing in the whole world would induce me to live under the same roof as Lord Windermere. You fill me with horror. There is something about you that stirs the wildest rage within me. And I know why you are here. My husband sent you to lure me back that I might serve as a blind to whatever relations exist between you and him.

MRS. ERLYNNE. Oh! You don't think that—you can't.

LADY WINDERMERE. Go back to my husband, Mrs. Erlynne. He belongs to you and not to me. I suppose he is afraid of a scandal. . . . But he had better prepare himself. He shall have a scandal. He shall have the worst scandal there has been in London for years. He shall see his name in every vile paper, mine on every hideous placard.

MRS. ERLYNNE. No—no—

LADY WINDERMERE. Yes! he shall. Had he come himself, I admit I would have gone back to the life of degradation you and he had prepared for me—I was going back—but to stay himself at home, and to send you as his messenger— oh! it was infamous—infamous.

MRS. ERLYNNE. Lady Windermere, you wrong me horribly —you wrong your husband horribly. He doesn't know you are here—he thinks you are safe in your own house. He thinks you are asleep in your own room. He never read the mad letter you wrote to him!

LADY WINDERMERE. Never read it!

MRS. ERLYNNE. No—he knows nothing about it.

LADY WINDERMERE. How simple you think me! (*Going to her.*) You are lying to me!

MRS. ERLYNNE. (*Restraining herself.*) I am not. I am telling you the truth.

LADY WINDERMERE. If my husband didn't read my letter, how is it that you are here? Who told you I had left the house you were shameless enough to enter? Who told you where I had gone to? My husband told you, and sent you to decoy me back.

MRS. ERLYNNE. Your husband has never seen the letter. I— saw it, I opened it. I—read it.

LADY WINDERMERE. (*Turning to her.*) You opened a letter of mine to my husband? You wouldn't dare!

MRS. ERLYNNE. Dare! Oh! to save you from the abyss into which you are falling, there is nothing in the world I would not dare, nothing in the whole world. Here is the letter. Your husband has never read it. He never shall read it. (*Going to fireplace.*) It should never have been written. (*Tears it and throws it into the fire.*)

LADY WINDERMERE. (*With infinite contempt in her voice and look.*) How do I know that that was my letter after all? You seem to think the commonest device can take me in!

MRS. ERLYNNE. Oh! why do you disbelieve everything I tell you! What object do you think I have in coming here, except . . . to save you from the consequence of a hideous mistake? That letter that is burning now *was* your letter. I swear it to you!

LADY WINDERMERE. (*Slowly.*) You took good care to burn it before I had examined it. I cannot trust you. You, whose whole life is a lie, how could you speak the truth about anything? (*Sits down.*)

MRS. ERLYNNE. (*Hurriedly.*) Think as you like about me— say what you choose against me, but go back, go back to the husband you love.

LADY WINDERMERE. (*Sullenly.*) I do *not* love him!

MRS. ERLYNNE. You do, and you know that he loves you.

LADY WINDERMERE. He does not understand what love is. He understands it as little as you do—but I see what you want. It would be a great advantage for you to get me back. Dear Heaven! what a life I would have then! Living at the mercy of a woman who has neither mercy nor pity in her, a woman whom it is an infamy to meet, a degradation to know . . . a woman who comes between husband and wife!

MRS. ERLYNNE. (*With a gesture of despair.*) Lady Windermere, Lady Windermere, don't say such terrible things. You don't know how terrible they are, . . . and how unjust. Listen, you must listen! Only go back to your husband, and I promise you never to communicate with him again on any pretext—never to see him—never to have anything to do with his life or yours. The money that he gave me, he gave me not through love, but through hatred, not in worship, but in contempt. The hold I have over him—

LADY WINDERMERE. (*Rising.*) Ah! you admit you have a hold!

MRS. ERLYNNE. Yes, and I will tell you what it is. It is his love for you, Lady Windermere.

LADY WINDERMERE. You expect me to believe that?

MRS. ERLYNNE. You must believe it! It is true. It is his love for you that has made him submit to—oh! call it what you like, tyranny, threats, anything you choose. But it is his love for you. His desire to spare you—shame, yes, shame and disgrace.

LADY WINDERMERE. What do you mean? You are insolent! What have I to do with you?

MRS. ERLYNNE. (*Humbly.*) Nothing. I know it—but I tell you that your husband loves you—that you may never meet with such love again in your whole life . . . and that if you throw it away, the day may come when you will starve for love and it will not be given to you, beg for love and it will be denied you— Oh! Arthur loves you!

LADY WINDERMERE. Arthur? And you tell me there is nothing between you?

MRS. ERLYNNE. Lady Windermere, before Heaven your husband is guiltless of all offense toward you! And I—I tell you that had it ever occurred to me that such a monstrous suspicion would have entered your mind, I would have died rather than have crossed your life or his—oh! died, gladly died! (*Moves away to sofa right.*)

LADY WINDERMERE. You talk as if you had a heart. Women like you have no hearts. . . . You are bought and sold.

MRS. ERLYNNE. (*Starts, with a gesture of pain. Then restrains herself, and comes over to where* LADY WINDERMERE *is sitting. As she speaks, she stretches out her hands toward her, but does not dare to touch her.*) Believe what you choose about me. I am not worth a moment's sorrow. But don't spoil your beautiful young life on my account! You don't know what may be in store for you, unless you leave this house at once. You don't know what it is to fall into the pit, to be despised, mocked, abandoned, sneered at—to be an outcast! . . . and all the while to hear the laughter, the horrible laughter of the world, a thing more tragic than all the tears the world has ever shed. You don't know what it is. One pays for one's sin, and then one pays again, and all one's life one pays. You must never know that.—As for me, if suffering be an expiation, then at this moment I have expiated all my faults, whatever they have been; for to-night you have made a heart in one who had it not, made it and broken it.—But let that pass. I may have wrecked my own life, but I will not let you wreck yours. . . . No! Go back, Lady Windermere, to the husband who loves you, whom you love. You have a child, Lady Windermere. Go back to that child. . . . He will require from you that you make his life fine, that you watch over him. . . . Back to your house, Lady Windermere—your husband loves you. He has never swerved for a moment from the love he bears you. But even if he had a thousand loves, you must stay with your child. If he was harsh to you, you must stay with your child. If he ill-treated you, you must stay with your child. If he abandoned you, your place is with your child. (LADY WINDERMERE *bursts into tears and buries her face in her hands. Rushing to her.*) Lady Windermere!

LADY WINDERMERE. (*Holding out her hands to her, helplessly, as a child might do.*) Take me home. Take me home.

DIALECT

THE BIG POND [1]

by

GEORGE MIDDLETON AND A. E. THOMAS

PIERRE, *an impoverished noble, has been brought to the United States by* MR. BILLINGS, *father of* BARBARA *who has fallen in love with* PIERRE. *Once here,* PIERRE *becomes a typical business man devoid of the romance* BARBARA *loved. In this speech* PIERRE *makes a last (and effective) plea for* BARBARA'S *affection. He includes in his audience a young American who is also in love with* BARBARA.

PIERRE. But you are not the only one who suffer for Miss Barbara. Me, *I* have suffered, too. I leave my home—my friends—I cross the Big Pond. Six days. Mon Dieu! Those six days! I can never forget them. Six days I lie on my back and wish I am *dead*. Then I work like the dog to please papa—and displease *her*—and I lecture about Belloni to a lot of stupid ladies— You think I don't suffer then— Oh, it is true I don't put my *umbrella* to bed—(*Stopping abruptly.*) Oh, it makes no difference if you love her or if I love her. The question is—does she love me *or* you. (*He turns to her.*) Mademoiselle, you love me—non? . . . Mademoiselle —I beg you, please. Je vous supplie, put from your mind all the unhappy things that have occur since we come here from France. Go back in your mind to the place we first met. We were happy like that, no? . . . Ah, oui— Eh bien. I am the same man. Only there is *one* difference. Then I was only a *poor* courier; I could not speak my love. Why that was you know very well. But *now* I am not poor any more. And so I *can* speak. I can tell the little Princess of my heart that I love her. And what does she say to me? [She say Non]. . . . Bien. Then I say to Mademoiselle good-bye. . . . I shall always love you—but I shall never see you again. (*He takes from his pocket the contract* BILLINGS *has given him.*) . . . You see: it is the contract your papa—give to me. (*He hands it to her.*) I am going home. . . . Yes, yes, yes. Can you not understand? (*With passion.*) What I care for America or papa or the business or the money or any damn thing in the world if you are not to be my wife? Que le diable— Rien nothing. Rien. (*Pulls himself up.*) Pardon. I do not mean to get excited. Non. I do not wish you to remember me like that. . . . Mon Dieu. You think I am going on in business? Non. You think I am going on like that—to see you all the time? At the house —on the street? "Bon jour, Mademoiselle; you are well to-day, I hope? Fine weather to-day, is it not? Au revoir, Mademoiselle"— To tear my heart in pieces like that! Mon Dieu, non. Thank you—and so I go New York to-morrow morning and at midnight—the *Mauretania* sails again. And now good-bye— (*He puts out his hand and takes hers and stoops over; as he kisses it the 'phone rings sharply. They pay no attention and it rings again. 'Phone again. He still holds her hand.*) . . . I am finish with the telephone. . . . I am finish with the office. . . . Eh? [Don't go?] . . . (*Advancing; not believing . . .*) Ah cherie? Cherie. . . . I love you! I love you! . . .

POLLY WITH A PAST [1]

by

GEORGE MIDDLETON AND GUY BOLTON

POLLY *is introduced to society posing as a French celebrity who has been rescued from drowning by a well-to-do young man. She tells his friends, with great gusto, how he saved her.*

POLLY. . . . Imagine to yourself: I am alone. . . . I go alone because I don't like to be stared at by everybody. You see, my bathing suit—eet ees just a trifle—a trifle . . . I am out of my depth. Ze waves are beeg like mountains. Ze undair-tow eet ees terrible. I scream. I 'ear a voice answair—"I come!" . . . I zee a man run down ze—ze plage—'ow you say?—*beach*—And 'e sweem to me. Just as 'e reach me a great wave sweep ovair 'im— . . . 'E sink—I sink—down —down—down through ze green watair! . . . Zen all go black. Zen somezing grabs me by ze leg. . . . Oh, 'e did not see what 'e was doing; 'e was nearly drowning heem-self. . . . 'E zink eet was my arm 'e 'ave 'old of. Zen 'e see 'is meestake and because 'e ees a gentleman 'e let go. I sink again. 'E dive for me like a fish and grab my hair wiz one hand and my neck by ze othair. 'E kick— (*Illustrating with arms.*) 'e tell me to kick. I kick. We come to ze top. 'E sweem wiz one arm; I sweem wiz ze othair. 'E drag me to shallow watair. 'E carry me to shore. 'E save my life. My 'ero. Et voilà!

THEY KNEW WHAT THEY WANTED [1]

by

SIDNEY HOWARD

TONY, *a California grape-grower has been looking around for a wife. He is telling his hopes to the priest,* FATHER MCKEE.

TONY. . . . I been lookin' all 'round here at all da womans in dees parish. I been lookin' evra place for twent' mile. Ees no good womans for wife here. Joe is told me 'bout evra one. Den I'm gone to Napa for look all 'round dere an' in Napa ees no better—ees just da same like here. So den I go down all da way to Frisco for look after wife an' I find my Amy. She is like a rose, all wilt'. You puttin' water on her an' she come out most beautiful. I'm goin' marry with my Amy, Padre, an' I don' marry with nobody else. She's been tellin' me she is no Cath'lic. I say, w'at I care? By an' by, maybe, if we bein' patient, we bringin' her in da church, an' showin' her da candles and da Madonna, all fix up good with flowers and da big tin heart, an' evrathing smellin' so prett' an' you preachin' verra loud an' da music an' evra-thing, maybe—by an' by— But now ees no matter. W'at I care? . . . I think you know verra good w'y [I no get mar-ried forty years ago!] Ees because I am no dam' fool.—W'en I'm young, I got nothing. I'm broke all da time, you re-member? I got no money for havin' wife. I don' want no wife for mak' her work all da time. Da's no good, dat. Da's mak' her no more young, no more prett'. Evrabody say Tony is crazy for no' havin' wife. I say Tony is no dam' fool. W'at is happen? Pro'ibish' is com'. Salute! . . . An' w'at I say? I say, "Ees dam' fool law. Ees dam' fool fellas for bein' scare' an' pullin' up da grape' for tryin' growin' som'thing different." W'at I'm doin'? I'm keep the grape, eh? I say, "I come in dees country for growin' da grape! God mak' dees country for growin' da grape! Ees not for pro'ibish' God mak' dees country. Ees for growin' da grape! Ees true? Sure ees true! (*Another glass of wine.*) An' w'at happen? Before pro'ibish' I sell my grape' for ten, maybe twelve dollar' da ton. Now I sell my grape' som'time one hundra dollar' da ton. Pro'ibish' is mak' me verra rich. (*An-other glass of wine.*) I got my fine house. I got Joe for bein' foreman. I got two men for helpin' Joe. I got one Chink for cook. I got one Ford car. I got all I want, evrathing, excep' only wife. Now I'm goin' have wife. Verra nice an' young an' fat. Not for work. No! For sit an' holdin' da hands and havin' kids. Three kids. (*He demonstrates the altitude of each.*) Antonio—Giuseppe—Anna— Da's like trees an' cows an' all good peoples. Da's fine for God an' evrabody! I tell you, Padre, Tony know w'at he want!

A TUNE OF A TUNE [1]

by

DAN TOTHEROH

SHEILA, *a young Irish girl, has brought into her mistress' house to shelter him from the rain,* EGAN *a peddler of children's toys. They are both quite wet from the storm.*

SHEILA. Egan, ye'd better hurry for it. There's another flash this minute an' the clouds will burst the next. Hurry now! Ye'll not be wantin' them jimcracks an' jacks-in-the-boxes to be takin' a bath from the sky.

EGAN. (*Behind her.*) Faith, an' it's comin' I am, Sheila O'Griffen.

(SHEILA *pushes open the little door and steps in. . . . She crosses to the hearth and begins shaking her bedraggled skirts at the prim fire.* EGAN, *the children's peddler, enters on tiptoes. . . . His tattered trouser legs are as sopped as* SHEILA's *skirt and his boots are as wet as her low shoes. Yet he hangs back from the fire.*)

SHEILA. Come up to the fire, Egan. Put down your toys an' come up. 'Tis a cold ye'll be gettin'.

EGAN. (*Putting down his tray on the floor and coming shyly up.*) Ain't ye afraid, Sheila O'Griffen, that 'tis mad Miss Pringle will be if she catches me? She likes not the floor to

[1] Copyright, 1928, by Samuel French (*in volume One Act Plays for Stage and Study, Fourth Series*).

be messed an' it's ye who knows an' it ain't for me to be tellin' ye.

SHEILA. Shoo! There's a bit of truth there but all she can do is storm an' it's doin' that already.

EGAN. (*Close to the fire.*) Ah, good it is. God made a wondrous thing in fire, Sheila.

SHEILA. Draw up a chair, Egan, an' make yourself to home.

EGAN. Ain't Miss Pringle somewhere above?

SHEILA. She be, an' most likely powdering her nose for the gentleman who comes here tonight.

EGAN. Then I'd not be likin' to sit down.

SHEILA. Shoo! What a coward ye are, Egan. Ye who knows the ways of the woods an' the bogs afraid of a small proper lady who has not the squeak or the bite of a field mouse. Sit down! Must I bend ye like one of your jointed dolls? (*She seats him in [the] big chair by taking him by the shoulders and pushing him down.*) There! Force ye to take comfort, I will. (*She sits on the hearth at his feet.*)

EGAN. Sure an' it was a surprise to find ye here in England, Sheila O'Griffen.

SHEILA. An' sure, Egan, 'twas the best luck in the world for me to find ye on this night.

EGAN. An' why this night of all nights?

SHEILA. Ah, it was sore vexed I was, Egan, an' sore vexed I still am. That's why I was out in the fields lettin' the rain drench me. I was awrestlin' with me problem when you comes along with your whistlin' an' drives it away, for the nonce, with that tune of a tune.

EGAN. That's the tune that me mother was born with an' I whistled to the cows when I was a lad an' drove 'em down to the lake where the fairies was. It's a tune that can make the grasses grow so full of magic it is.

SHEILA. Faith, it's a tune of a tune. It's a tune for the stars an' the wind an' the moon an' the folks who is hungry for freedom! (*She stretches herself out on the hearthstone and gives way to a long drawn sigh.*)

EGAN. Why are ye troubled this night, Sheila O'Griffen?

SHEILA. (*After a moment's pause.*) Mr. Barstow it is that's troublin' me, Egan.

EGAN. Not the rich Mr. Barstow what has the big house with the towers an' the gardens with the peacocks?

SHEILA. The very same, an' he please ye, Egan.

EGAN. He don't please me. His dogs has many's the time chased me away from his gates. An' what's he done to ye, Sheila?

SHEILA. It's not what he's done. It's what he's up to be doin'.

EGAN. Faith, an' what's that?

SHEILA. He's up to proposin' marriage, that's what he's up to.

EGAN. Him—?

SHEILA. This very night he's up to it. Today, through his hedge I saw his maid, Tillie, apickin' rosemary in the hot-house, a very little ye may be sure, but it's a true sign. She'll mix it with phlox an' her master will present it to me like it was orchids, sayin' all the while to himself, "She's a lucky lass to be gettin' it from Mr. Barstow." (*She pounds on the hearth with her clenched fist.*)

EGAN. Faith, an' ye'll never be happy with the likes of him, Sheila O'Griffen. You're a lass of the wild Irish lakes an' forests an' (*Bending down to her.*) the fairies! (*He reaches out to touch her hair but she springs up.*)

SHEILA. (*Her eyes on the fire.*) Shoo now, Egan, there was a queer tappin' last night on me window an' I first thought it was the vine that climbs, but then it was stronger an' louder and more, (*Her voice is down in her shoes.*) more insistent.

EGAN. (*Excited.*) An' did I not say it? You're a lass of the fairies. 'Twas them a-callin' ye.

SHEILA. Sometimes I think a silk dress an' a garden with peacocks would be to me likin' an' then, under me hair, I begin to ache. Oh, Egan, how I ache, under me hair, on each side of me head.

EGAN. (*Rising.*) Ache? Ah, that's a fair warnin'.

SHEILA. Yes, under me hair on each side of me head. . . .

EGAN. (*Hearing and scared.*) That's Miss Pringle! Sure, an' she mustn't find me here.

SHEILA. An' why not? She's a Christian woman an' a Christian woman cannot refuse a poor peddler a bit of a fire, a bit of a seat, an' a bit of shelter from the storm. It's the Bible that teaches it.

EGAN. (*Moving toward his tray and the door.*) Sure' an' if it's just the same to you I'd rather go. There's the ale house down by the church.

SPRING O' THE YEAR [1]

by

W. H. ROBERTSON

JAMIE, *a Scotch lad, feels the call to make his living in America, and after church, he tactfully weaves the conversation to his will, while talking to his father.*

JAMIE. . . . Queer notions women have—even Mither at times. . . .

WILLIAM. . . . Aye, and men and lads—all queer notions—at times. But they're no so queer after all as ye come older.

JAMIE. . . . Aye, ye're right, Faither! . . .

WILLIAM. (*A little startled.*) Eh?

JAMIE. (*Sits.*) Queer notions, all o' us—I've one noo—

WILLIAM. (*Quickly craning back to look toward kitchen door.*) Aye and your mither has one—she must wash the dishes just at this time and no other—

JAMIE. But whit I mean is—my notion's no queer to me, but it might be queer to ye and Mither—that is, at first it might— . . . Faither, how old was Uncle Angus when he went to America?

WILLIAM. Old enough to ken he shud have stayed by his mither. . . .

JAMIE. And how old was that, Faither?

WILLIAM. Twenty-four was Angus.—

JAMIE. . . . I'm twenty-four.—Uncle Angus must be aboot sixty noo—am I right, Faither? . . . Sixty. It's taken him aboot thirty-six years. . . . First a printer in a printworks. Then a foreman. Then a super. Then a partner and treasurer in his ain works. Then in the banks—whit's this ye call them?—Directors!—Thirty-six years . . . Faither! I'm thinkin' I can do as guid as him!

WILLIAM. Aye, and all ye'd need wud be a horn and a guid breath to blaw it!

JAMIE. But, Faither, there's the clippings from the journals Uncle Angus sent us—!

WILLIAM. (*With a toss of his head.*) Blatherskite!

JAMIE. And the one tellin' aboot him being a Director—it has his photo in it—

WILLIAM. Some folks likes their pictures in the journals where everybody can gape and gawp at them! A bawdy business havin' your ain private face made public of!

JAMIE. Weel, I suppose when ye're a bank director—

WILLIAM. (*Sharply to* JAMIE.) Mind this, Jamie! Angus had a very clever way aboot him—he cud pull the wool over the Americans' eyes but he cudna fool me. Director! (*He slumps down in his chair again.*) I've no a very high opinion of the bank!

JAMIE. Weel, maybe they're no very big banks he's in, but Curley Noble wrote his mither that Uncle Angus was a big mon in Rhode Island.

WILLIAM. Pisht! Dominie Henderson tellt me 'tis an awful wee place that Rhode Island! Ye cud lift it wie your twa fingers and drop it into Scotland and Scotland wudna ken 'twas here at all!

JAMIE. (*Rises and goes to* WILLIAM.) But it canna be so awful small for Curley Noble and Charlie MacDonald baith got jobs at once they'd landed. . . . And ye mind whit Uncle Angus wrote last December—aboot the shortage o' guid printworks men and that I'd have a braw job and high pay if I'd come—

WILLIAM. But ye didna ken he'd wrote the manager of your printworks first to find out aboot ye and when he'd heard aboot your fine work, then he wrote us— Angus was never the mon to cast his line till he was sure whit fish was in the pond!

JAMIE. But, Faither, d'ye no see with my character sent on ahead o' me, my road's clear—I've only to step out on it!

WILLIAM. (*After looking at him sharply.*) But last December ye said ye wudna go!

JAMIE. (*Turning away.*) Aye, then—but since—. . . . Oh, Faither, dinna think I've no fought it! For three weeks I've fought it day and night! I've shut my lugs to it; I've whistled till my mouth was weary tryin' to drive the thought from my mind; but it's no guid! It's like a voice callin 'and callin'—it fills my head so I canna think o' naith-ing besides gettin' to America—makin' my start whilest I'm young and have the chancet!

THE SCARING OFF OF TEDDY DAWSON [1]

by

HAROLD BRIGHOUSE

The living room of a small East End house.
. . . At the table POLLY BETTESWORTH *is ironing. . . . Her husband* ANDREW *throws open the door center and enters rapidly. . . . He is a navvy, . . . and is in his shirt sleeves, having been to the nearest public for the supper beer, which is in a large jug in his hand. . . .*

ANDREW. (*Angrily.*) Where's our Liza?

POLLY. What do yer want 'er for?

ANDREW. (*Closing door.*) I'm goin' to tan 'er 'ide for 'er.

POLLY. What's to do? (*Calmly continuing ironing.*)

ANDREW. (*Crossing to door left.*) I'll put beer in back to keep cool an' then I'll tell yer. (*Opens left door, leaves jug inside and closes door again.*) Now, do yer know wot I've bin 'earing in the *Bluebell* abart our Liza?

POLLY. Tell me.

ANDREW. Liza's started courtin'! That's wot that whistlin's bin as we've bin 'earing so much lately.

[1] Copyright, 1911, by Samuel French, Limited.

POLLY. (*Stopping ironing.*) Courtin'! At 'er age?

ANDREW. It's Gawd's truth. Wait while I catch the bloke wot's after 'er. I'll skin 'im alive.

POLLY. (*Sitting.*) Liza courtin'! I don't know wot things is comin' to nowadays. Young girls are gettin' a set of forward hussies that haven't hardly laid by their skipping-ropes afore they're thinkin' they're ould enough to get wed. I fancied we'd brought 'er up different to that.

ANDREW. I'll fancy 'er—'er an' 'er fancy man, an' all. I'll teach 'im to come round 'ere whistling for our Liza. We ain't partin' with Liza yet. She's the only 'un left to us now.

POLLY. Yus. T'other girls went off a sight too young. Fust Martha an' then Sally must be havin' their blokes an' gettin' wed. But I didn't think it of Liza. She's kept 'er mouth shut. Them quiet 'uns are always deep.

ANDREW. Nature 'ull 'ave its way with 'em so what you do. (*Fiercely.*) But I'll spoil this chap's little game. I don't like 'im, not arf like 'im I don't.

POLLY. Who is 'e?

ANDREW. Teddy Dawson's 'is name.

POLLY. (*Rising.*) Teddy Dawson! Wild as they make 'em that chap is. 'E's after no good with Liza.

ANDREW. I'll mar 'is good looks if I catch 'im. 'E'll not be so keen on comin' an' whistlin' at street corner like a canary in a fit. And I'll give Liza the taste of my strap an' all.

POLLY. (*Firmly.*) Yer'll not touch the girl, Andrew.

ANDREW. Who won't?

POLLY. I'll give 'er a piece of my mind.

ANDREW. An' I'll give 'er a piece of my belt.

POLLY. Yer won't. Me an' yer didn't arsk our old 'uns for

leave to start courtin'. Liza 'ull go the way o' all flesh when 'er time comes.

ANDREW. Yus, but 'er time ain't come yet, not by a bloomin' long chalk, an' I'll make 'er know it.

POLLY. Yer leave Liza to me. Yer can do wot yer loike with Teddy Dawson an' welcome.

ANDREW. I'll make 'im wish 'e'd never bin born.

POLLY. I dunno. Yer've tried that road twice—with Martha's man an' Sally's.

ANDREW. (*Reminiscently, gloating.*) I did an' all. They didn't 'ave much of a larky toime courtin'. I put strap abart both of 'em more than once.

POLLY. An' they only came the more.

ANDREW. Yus. They was spunky fellers. This bloke 'ull not take it that way. 'E'll cut an' run.

POLLY. I'm not so sure it's the right road to scare 'em off.

ANDREW. It's the only road I knows of. Do yer think yer knows a better?

POLLY. I dunno as I do. Hush! There's Liza comin' downstairs. Now, keep yer mouth shut till I've had my say.

THE MAN WHO DIED AT TWELVE O'CLOCK [1]

by

PAUL GREEN

On the day before their wedding, CHARLIE *hesitatingly conveys to* SALLY *that something is not entirely as it was planned.* SALLY *is working on a devil's costume for* CHARLIE

[1] Copyright, 1927, by Samuel French (*in volume One Act Plays for Stage and Study, Second Series*).

to wear in a play, and trying to dispel whatever is bother-ing CHARLIE—*all she can gather is that it concerns her* UNCLE JANUARY. *The three characters are Negro.*

SALLY. . . . Cain't see why you worry. We three's gwine live on heah happy as you please. Look at dis devil's costyume you gwine to wear to-night in de play. Booh! (*She suddenly whirls towards him, holding up a long red tight-fitting suit, horns, tail, and hoofs attached. Two terrifying eyes and a wide grinning mouth glare out at him.*)

CHARLIE. (*Starting back in alarm.*) Lawd! Hyuh, hyuh, don't shake dat thing at me!

SALLY. Ho, ho, ho! I sho' has made a' awful critter, ain't I?

CHARLIE. (*Coming up and touching it gingerly.*) Lawd, Lawd, dat's a turble sight. Reckon 'twon't th'ow de folkses into fits when I comes stepping, crost de stage wid dat thing on?

SALLY. (*Sitting down with the garment in her lap and beginning to sew again.*) I got to finish dis left-hand hawn; den you kin take it on wid you. I was gwine have it all done and complete foh you if you hadn't come early. Mought a-put it on and skeahed you wid it.

CHARLIE. Yeh, and I'd a-tore up de road gwine 'way from heah. Wouldn't had no devil in de dialogue to-night, been a-roosting in de swamp. (*He sits down forlornly and watches her sew.*) You's raght handy wid a needle, ain't you?

SALLY. I is dat. And, boy, I'se gwine make you mo' shirts and things dan a few. And knit! I kin knit, too. (*Jokingly.*) You better not think of th'owing me over heah at de last. Ain't many gals good at housekeeping lak me.

CHARLIE. (*Uneasily.*) Hyuh, hyuh, don't talk lak dat. It hurts me worse'n it do you to think o' putting it off.

SALLY. Putting it off? We ain't gwine put it off.

CHARLIE. (*Wretchedly.*) Don't seem no way out'n it.

SALLY. Way out'n whut?

CHARLIE. Everything's busted to pieces, dat's how.

SALLY. Is! How come?

CHARLIE. You don't know whah Uncle Jan is, do you?

SALLY. (*With satisfaction.*) Hunh, dat I do. In de bottom chopping his cawn. He's off dis mawning wid his hoe by sunrise. Needn't worry 'bout him.

CHARLIE. (*Bitterly*). In de bottom! He's in de bottom of a drunk, de old fool!

SALLY. (*Incredulously.*) Hyuh, don't be trying to skeah *me* now.

CHARLIE. Trying! I wisht I had to try.

SALLY. Dat's too serious to be joking 'bout. Tell me de truf.

CHARLIE. I'se telling you de truf. He mought a-gone off dis mawning wid a hoe, but when I come by Luke's sto' up de road few minutes ago dere he sot on a box wid a co'-cola bottle in his hand, beating and a-flamming and a-cussing in de wind.

SALLY. (*With a wail.*) O Lawd!

CHARLIE. When he seed me a-coming, he fell to lambanging and telling 'em to let him make at me. Dey had to hold him back or I'd a-had to cave in his haid. Dere's yo' new-bawn lamb and follower of Jesus foh you. He's gut fed up on pizen liquor. He was so mad at me dat he 'gun to spit and spew all over de flo'. Said he's coming raght on home and shoot me full of holes if he found me heah. (*Wrath-fully.*) Hurry and git dat last hawn fixed, I gut to be moving. Lawd, I won't feel lak cutting up no shines to-night.

SALLY. (*Her hands lying limp in her lap.*) O Lawd, whut

kin we do? (*A sob breaks in her voice.*) And heah we was wid everything fixed foh good.

CHARLIE. He 'bused me black and blue in de face. Said all I wanted was yo' money and dat I'd never git it. He had it hid whah nobody could find it and he's gwine let Luke have it to put in his sto'. (*Standing up from his chair and clenching his fist.*) Wisht to Gohd I had dat Luke Ligon heah in dis room, I'd frail him to deaf.

SALLY. We gut to do something, I tell you. Dat Luke git his claws on my money and dat's de end of it. (*They both sit thinking, wretched.*) When Grandpap comes cain't you'n me shet him up and make him give it up to us or tell us whah it is?

CHARLIE. Yeh, and dat man'll cut you all to pieces wid a knife. He's mean and he's full o' liquor. And 'sides you ain't twenty-one. Dey'd have de law on bofe of us. (SALLY *gets up and moves nervously around the room.*) Gimme dat costyume and lemme leave. Wisht to de good Gohd he'd a seed de devil dressed in dis suit in his vision, and I reckon he'd a-not been back in his weekedness so soon!

SALLY. (*Stopping in her walk.*) Kin you see him coming? I gut a idee. (CHARLIE *goes to the window and looks out.*)

CHARLIE. (*Excitedly.*) Yeh, yeh, yonder he comes down de hill and walking all over de road. Gimme dat and lemme git away.

SALLY. Wait a speck. (*She wrinkles her brow in thought.*)

CHARLIE. Why foh?

SALLY. I believe I got a way to fix him.

CHARLIE. Hurry up. How you mean?

SALLY. (*Picking up the suit.*) Skeah him, dat's how.

CHARLIE. Wid dat?

SALLY. Yeh, I b'lieves we kin do it.

CHARLIE. He mought shoot us.

SALLY. I'll hide his gun. (*She runs to the corner, takes the gun, unloads it, and throws it under the bed.*) Now gimme de shells. (*She gets a box of shells from the wash-stand, opens the window at the right and throws them out.*)

CHARLIE. Whut you mean to do?

SALLY. (*Growing excited.*) Listen. Look at dat dere clock, neah 'bout twelve. Well, when twelve straks Grandpap is gwine die.

CHARLIE. Die? We—we ain't gwine kill him, is we? Naw suh, I ain't—Sally you,—

SALLY. I hopes we won't kill him, but he's gwine think his time's come.

CHARLIE. (*Turning quickly back to the window.*) Oh— Hurry up wid yo' plans den, yonder he is now down by de branch place.

SALLY. (*Breathlessly.*) It des flashed on me lak a streak. It's dis. He had de vision dat he's gwine die some day at twelve when de devil comes foh him. Dat's whut de devil told him. Well, when he comes in heah to lie down and sleep off his drunk I's gwine set up a monstrous heap o' wailing and screeching sorter lak I has to do in de dialogue, 'cepting worse. You be shet up in de entry dressed in dis heah suit. I'll skeah him to deaf wid my talk 'bout signs and sich, and den when de clock straks twelve you come in to git him. Lawd, he'll git religion dis day, see'f he don't.

CHARLIE. How you know we kin do all dat? He might git something and brain me wid it, I tells you.

SALLY. Dat he won't. He's gwine be skeahed worse'n he's ever been. And he'll cough up dat money, and tell all his sins, and 'fo' he's got straight ag'in, we'll be all fixed. And he ain't never gwine know it wa'n't de devil adder him. Boy, we'll sho' have all de under-holt yit.

CHARLIE. (*Staring at her.*) Lawd, Lawd, you's de sharpest gal I ever did see in dis world.

SALLY. Dis heah's de time to be sharp if we's gwine git married to-morrow. Now, hyuh. When you come in wid yo' devil's suit on, you talk to him, ax him all sorts of question. He'll tell everything. (*Bubbling over with excitement.*) Yeh, yeh, we gut him whah we want him at last. And I'll make out all de time dat I cain't see devil or nothing. (*Coming up to him and hugging him in courageous ecstasy.*) We gwine have some fun out'n him. Adder today I bet my hat he'll be a shouting Christian.

CHARLIE. (*Warming to the game.*) All raght, honey, dis heah's de time. I'll stick to you. And talk 'bout cutting a rust at dat schoolhouse? I's gwine make a to-do wid dat old man whut is one!

SALLY. Now you slip in de entry and shet de do' and doll up. We gwine have a sober man on our hands in a few minutes. Hurry, hurry, dere he is coming by de woodpile.

ONE SUNDAY AFTERNOON [1]

by

JAMES HAGAN

A beer garden of twenty-five years ago, used at this moment as a picnic ground for a retail merchants association. MRS. OBERSTATTER *and* MRS. SCHITZENMEYER *meet.*

MRS. O. Wie gehts, Mrs. Schnitzenmeyer, I see you are here.

MRS. S. Wie gehts, Mrs. Oberstatter—yah I am here. Ach du lieber Gott! Such a crowd I vish I vas home.

---

[1] Copyright, 1930, 1933, by James Hagan.

MRS. O. Yah? Sitzen ze zicht—

MRS. S. Yah. Already I tell Otto, dot's my husband—he works by the brewery house—already I say "Otto, I vish I vas home"—

.   .   .   .

MRS. O. Alvays such a crowd like this when the retail merchants give a picnic. Every year it is the same. My husband already got me six tickets for the raffles.

.   .   .   .

MRS. S. So!

MRS. O. Your husband und you vell?

MRS. S. Yah. Und your family?

MRS. O. Ach! Dey has grown so tall, at once. Lena is as tall as me.

MRS. S. Yah!

MRS. O. Yah. Children grow so fast today. Yesterday I say to my husband, "Fritz, I say— By und by Papa, Louie and Johnnie be as tall as you"— He say "Hah?"—I say "Yah."

.   .   .   .

MRS. O. You see the fight, Mrs. Schnitzenmeyer?

MRS. S. Nein. Vho is it dot makes the fight?

MRS. O. Dot Grimes boy is von! . . . Ach! Dot Grimes boy! Such a bully—

MRS. S. Such a loafer! Ach du lieber Gott!

MRS. O. Already he should be run out of town. My husband Fritz told me about it.

MRS. S. Such peace und quiet at a picnic und den dot loafer—

MRS. O. Dere vas a gang und one of them say something to the Grimes boy— . . . Van dat boy say something to the Grimes boy—the Grimes boy make out he hit him in the face und the udder boy fall down on the ground.

MRS. S. Ach du lieber himmel! . . . Such a big bully.

. . . .

MRS. O. Mr. Schneider run up and say "Vun more fight und out you go."

MRS. S. Good for Mr. Schneider—

MRS. O. Yah—dot is good for Mr. Schneider.

. . . .

MRS. S. By und by we vatch dem hit the nigger on the head for a nickel, yah?

MRS. O. Yah.

JEREMIAD [1]

by

JOSEPHINE HENRY WHITEHOUSE

REBECCA BRAUNSTEIN, *the mother of two ambitious daughters, longs for Hester street where she had sympathetic, but not such wealthy neighbors. She finds her confidant in* MARY, *the Irish maid.*

REBECCA. . . . How happen it you ain't gone, Mary? . . . Nu, . . . out with you. (REBECCA *makes an outward motion with her hands.*) No more talkings. . . . I ain't forget to cook, Mary. No more klatsch. Nu, out with you. . . . (RE-BECCA *approaches table and starts unpacking basket.*) Herring—herring like you yet, Mary? . . . Oi weh is me! It's long as I taste good herring. Ach! the days what we live by Hester street. Nu, we pay for style as I don't like, for help what won't work—for marble hall—— . . . Oi! I wear shoes by me too tight, corsets who squeezes me to pieces—I stand by the dress-maker all day so I please Leah and Esther. Oi weh! I ain't my own master yet. I can't have jelly by my tea, Mary. Na, it don't go by America.

[1] Copyright, 1926, by Samuel French.

(*Pause.*) Hester street make me lonesome—them was the days—something every minute doing, ain't it? I look out the window and talk by Mrs. Gutowitz. Oi! I die by the quiet in West End Avenue. No money had Popper and me but what come by the Lodge. Nu, I go to school by my girls, Leah and Esther. (*Pause.*) You wait, Mary—— . . . My head—— (*She holds it in her hands a moment.*) Such a buzz. Mommer, don't eat by your saucer in one ear. Mommer, don't make noise by your soup; the other— Mommer, don't pick your teeth. Like phonograph all the time. Oi weh is me! . . . And it's change by you I would, Mary! . . . It ain't so good by me like they say—all alone by mir. Nu, I go by a party. Na, it's uncomfortable and quick I wants to be home before I done it wrong like Esther and Leah wants. Peoples thinks as you come by moneys it gets happy. It ain't, Mary, it ain't. . . . I seen a flat by Hester street. When Esther and Leah come by husbands already I go live that place.

BOYS WILL BE BOYS [1]

by

Charles O'Brien Kennedy
Founded on Irvin S. Cobb's short story

peep o'day, *a beloved old vagabond, has suddenly come into a large inheritance. The town's most crafty lawyer tries to get a girl to pose as* peep's *niece, have him declared insane, and get control of the money. The kindly* judge *realizes that* peep's *actions (such as taking the whole town to the circus, or buying a watermelon patch and letting the youngsters think they are "hooking" the melons), are only his dreams come true, allows* peep *to speak for himself.*

[1] Copyright, 1918, by Charles O'Brien Kennedy and Irvin S. Cobb. Copyright, 1925, by Samuel French Inc.

PEEP. Thank yer, Jedge—nobody seems ter understand—
'cept Miss Lucy and Mr. Tom and mebbe some of the little
kiddies hyah. I hed a puppose—a puppose in everythin' I
did. There's some hyah as knows how I was raised and
fetched up—My Maw and Paw died when I was little
more'n a baby, so I was brung up in the old county
po'house. Cayn't remember the time when I didn't hev to
work hard for jest my board and keep—while other boys
wuz goin' ter school and playin' games and sich—I hed ter
work. I never knowed what it was till a while ago to hev
my fill o' bananas and candy and sich knick-knacks.—
All my life I've craved ter wear a pair of red-topped boots
with brass toes onter 'em, same as I seed other boys wearin'
in the winter time when I was out yonder at the poorhouse
—just a little feller—but a-wearin' a pair of men's cast-off
shoes with rags wrapped round the toes ter keep the snow
frum comin' in the cracks.—More'n oncet I got my toes
frost-bit through wearin' them kind o' shoes—that's why I
bought a pair o' red-topped boots the fust time I hed the
price—and I got a heap of pleasure out o' doin' it, too. Ever
sinct I was a boy I've been wantin' ter go ter a circus, but
till terday I never hed no chanct.—Lots of the little
fellers here hedn't never seen one nuther, and I didn't want
no child in this town ter grow up to be my age 'thout seein'
at least *one* circus, so I sent 'em all—and I paid the bills.
—Some folks might think I wuz extravagant—well,
mebbe I wuz—but the little fellers wuz happy, so I reckin
I got my money's worth.—They may be bigger circuses
than this one wuz, but frum what I hears I don't see how
they could be any better.—I never said nuthin' like this
ter nobody afore cos I was afraid folks wouldn't understand, and would jest nachally laff at me.—All these
years I've had a hankerin' inside me—I've had a hankerin'
ter be a boy and do the things a boy does—to do the things
I wuz cheated outer doin' when I was a boy and oughter

bin a-doin' 'em—so when this money cum ter me so sud-
denlike I started out ter make my dream come true—and I
done it. I reckin that's why you think I'm crazy.—Well,
I don't regret it none, and if I had ter do it all over again
I'd do it just the same. You all say I'm in my second childhood— The way I look at it, a feller can't be in his
second childhood 'lessen he's hed his *just* childhood, and I
figger I was cheated plum outer mine. Every man is entitled
ter bein' a boy oncet in his life. I'm more'n sixty years old,
but I'm tryin' ter be one afore it's too late. I don't know
what the law says is the right time fer bein' one—only
some fellers don't git no chanct to be boys when they is
boys—so when the chanct does come ter be boys—they jest
goes and bes 'em.

ROADSIDE [1]

by

Lynn Riggs

TEXAS, *the speaker, is a son of the state whose name he
bears. He is a sort of south-western Robin Hood, full of
the glorious humor of his kind, ready for whatever comes
along. At present he is talking to* HANNIE, *whom he meets
after breaking jail.*

TEXAS. I wasn't borned in the ordinary way. (*Waggishly.*)
I'd a-thought you'd knowed that by lookin' at me—
(*Lyrically.*) No, sir! I'm gonna tell you jist the way it was
— Way out on the Texas prairie jist this side the tall moun-
tains set a small cabin made outa oak. And in that cabin, set
a man and womern with a growed gal as purty as purty

could be! Name was Liza. Mornin' come, she'd hop on her
pony to ride the range, her old pap and mammy a-runnin'
after her to stop her. "Come on back, Liza," they'd say—
"the plains is full of coyotes. Them big old growly mountain b'ars has started to sharpen up their spring teeth."
And seein' she didn't answer, they'd say, "Don't go fur,
then, and come back soon." And away she'd go! Greased
lightnin'! Dynamite on wings! Her pony stretched hisself
out like a tentpole headed West! When she was seven mile
and half away, she'd stop and look around. Now a funny
thing! She had rid into a valley whur a river used to flow
in the year 1. The tall grasses stood up like trees. A quair
kind of a roarin' like lions come from some'eres among the
tall grass. She'd git off her horse, look around, suspicious
like, and go into that valley on foot. She'd stay all day. Who
did she see thar? Whut did she do thar? Fer it soon was
evident's the nose on yer face, she was gonna produce a
infant. Who was its pappy? Whut kind of a roarin', hell-
shootin', brawny big mountain of a man was she a-
consortin' with? Somebody! With a whole valley fer his
house, and a sky fer a roof over him! A nameless wonder of
a giant with all out of doors to call his front room. A secret
man that roared when he talked and shuck the ground like
a earthquake rumblin'! Fin'lly one night—Liza lay in her
pappy's cabin. Wild hosses come a-nickerin' and trompin'
around. Great big b'ars as high as hills begin to growl
sump'n fierce. All of a sudden, there was a crash and a
bang and a clatter! Thunder and hail and lightnin', hell
f'ar and brimstone! The cabin whur Liza lay cracked itself
wide open from stem to stern, beam-end to beam-end, hind-
end to gullet! And when the smoke cleared away, out *I*
stepped, full-size, dressed to kill, in a ten-gallon hat, boots
and chaps, a gun in ary hand, and both guns a-poppin'!
And that's how I got started!

THE SQUALL [1]

by

JEAN BART

The threatening gypsy, EL MORO, *has been turned away by the Mendez family, in their pity for* NUBI, *a slave girl who has asked their protection. When the coast is clear,* NUBI *is brought out of hiding, and thanks her benefactress.*

NUBI. (*Crosses; gets on her knees before* DOLORES; *kisses the hem of her dress.*) Senora, the good God bless you many, many times because you have pity. [Nubi] is your slave. . . . [My name] it means "cloud" in Gitano. The night when I was born a cloud covered the moon—and passed. . . . It was Esora who told me. Esora is the mother of the tribe—she is wise! And old, like the world. She teach me how to read the past in stars. . . . [But] the future. Ha! . . . The Future, that is God's secret, Senor[a]—no one can know the future. . . . June has come fifteen times since I be born, and sixteen times the leaves they fall. . . .

. . . I not be hungry—I not want anything—only to stay here very "leeetle," very "leeetle" in corner. Tonight when gypsies are far away then I will go, Senora. (*She looks up with a bewitching smile.*)—perhaps!—maybe! I can stay here and work—maybe the good Senora have pity and keep me as servant. . . . Oh, yes, Senora—I'll be very happy—I work for you all day, all night. I work in fields, in house. I carry water from fountain. Please, Senora, you not send me away. . . .

. . . (*Kissing the hem of her dress.*) Senora—Nubi will be your slave—always. . . . (*Closes her eyes, visualizing the future. Slowly.*) Yes, Senora—yes. Some day—I'll be very, very happy. . . . (NUBI *raises her head and listens, motionless. Her voice falls to a terrified whisper.*) Listen— listen—the Gitanos! . . . (*Whispers.*) Yes. It is the farewell song of the tribe—listen. . . . (NUBI *remains on her knees, as though transfixed or hypnotized. . . . Very softly, her melodious voice gradually rising with the song.*) Always the gypsies sing a weird and sad song, always. On the long roads when their feet bleed they sing. When they are hungry, in misery, they sing. But the girl the gypsies steal never sings, never—always she weep and waits for day when she be free. (*Realizing that she is free at last. Changes mood completely.*) Now—Nubi she is free. She has someone who pities—someone who loves. (. . . NUBI *looks up and listens, then runs to center door; addresses the caravan with savage joy.*) Go, gypsies—go—for always Nubi will see you no more, Gitanos. No more I'll cry because you beat me, Moro. No more my feet will bleed on the long roads. (*Wildly.*) To hell with you—Gitanos!! (*She breaks into a wild, mocking laugh.*) . . .

BOOK LIST AND INDEX

BOOK LIST

Nicholson, Kenyon. Torch Song. $2.00

O'Neil, George. American Dream. $2.00

O'Neill, Eugene. Anna Christie. $2.50

Priestley, J. B. Dangerous Corner. $2.00

Riggs, Lynn. Roadside. $2.00

Robertson, W. H. Spring o' the Year. 75¢

Rostand, Edmond. Cyrano de Bergerac. In "Plays for College Theatre" ed. Garrett Leverton. $4.00

Shakespeare, William. As You Like It. 25¢
                    Julius Caesar. 25¢
                    The Merchant of Venice. 25¢
                    Romeo and Juliet. 25¢

Sheridan, Richard Brinsley. The School for Scandal. 25¢

Totheroh, Dan. A Tune of a Tune (one-act). In "One Act Plays for Everyone." $2.00

van Druten, John. There's Always Juliet. $2.00

Whitehouse, Josephine Henry. Jeremiad (one-act). 30¢

Wilde, Oscar. The Importance of Being Earnest. 75¢
                    Lady Windermere's Fan. 75¢

Copies of all plays listed above may be purchased through Samuel French, 25 W. 45th St., or the Drama Book Shop 48 W. 52nd St., New York City.

INDEX

(According to Titles of Plays)

137